The Rainbow in the Storm

Millennial Mind Publishing
An imprint of American Book Publishing
5442 So. 900 East, #146
Salt Lake City, UT 84117-7204
www.american-book.com
Printed in the United States of America on acid-free paper.

The Rainbow in the Storm: Finding Hope Where There Isn't Any

Designed by Jana Rade, design@american-book.com

Publisher's Note: *American Book Publishing relies on the author's integrity of research and attribution; each statement has not been investigated to determine if it has been accurately made. The author and publisher specifically disclaim any responsibility for any liability, loss, or risk, personal or otherwise, which is incurred as a consequence, directly or indirectly, of the use and application of any of the contents of this book. In such situations where medical, legal, or other professional services may apply, please seek the advice of such professionals directly.*

Library of Congress Cataloging-in-Publication Data
Chamberlain, Diane K.
 The rainbow in the storm : finding hope where there isn't any / by Diane K. Chamberlain.
   p. cm.
 ISBN-13: 978-1-58982-535-2 (alk. paper)
 ISBN-10: 1-58982-535-7 (alk. paper)
 1. Hope--Religious aspects--Christianity. 2. Hope--Biblical teaching. 3. Consolation--Biblical teaching. 4. Bible--Quotations. 5. Chamberlain, Diane K. I. Title.
 BV4905.3.C43 2009
 242'.4--dc22
                          2009004346

Special Sales
These books are available at special discounts for bulk purchases. Special editions, including personalized covers, excerpts of existing books, and corporate imprints, can be created in large quantities for special needs. For more information e-mail info@american-book.com.

The Rainbow in the Storm
Finding Hope Where There Isn't Any

By Diane K. Chamberlain

Acknowledgements

First of all, I thank Jesus for bringing me through a lot of pain and heartache. Over the years, You have become my best friend and I could never repay You for the true love You've shown me. When there were rough moments and the storms became fierce, in some small way, I knew You were there, watching over me.

I thank my husband for always being there in my life. We have faced many raging storms in our life together, but there was never a time that you left me alone. I thank you for the love and encouragement you always gave me and even though there were many times I couldn't believe in myself, you always did. God has used you as a very strong instrument in my life and I love you for that.

I thank my Mother for teaching me about Jesus. I thank her for the unselfish love and care she showed me as I went through many painful surgeries. I am so thankful to have a Mother like you!

To my Dad, who is now in Heaven...soon there will come a day when I will see you again. The scars will be gone and there won't be any more pain. There will never be any crutches, walkers, or canes in Heaven, and when I see you, I will be able to run into your arms for the first time.

To my brothers and sister, Vern, Don, and Linda, I thank you for understanding the pain I went through as a young girl. Your love and support has become very special throughout the years.

To those out there that I have known, along with others that I've never met, I give you these beautiful words as a gift from God and me. I pray that each word will bring hope, strength and new growth into your lives in the same way God has blessed me. My prayer for you is that God's hope will help you through the discouraging moments.

Foreword

As a young child that should have enjoyed a fun, exciting, and normal childhood, Diane K. Chamberlain's life was anything but that. While her friends were riding their bicycles and playing typical childhood games, Diane lived in a much different world, a world of extreme physical pain and eventual sheer disgust that robbed her of much of that childhood. During those formative years Diane had no way of knowing that God was grooming her for something much greater, something that would far surpass her earthly problems.

Even as a young Bible believing Christian, Diane could not have foreseen how God would use her life to be an instrument of incredible inspiration, encouragement, hope, and determination to individuals around the world.

In an honest attempt to convey much of the physical, emotional, mental, and spiritual pain she went through, Diane has delivered a quality book that exalts our Lord, Jesus Christ. She has not sugared coated, nor toned down the hurtful and disgusting situations she has had to suffer through. Instead she has boldly told us how big God is and how He was always there for her. Hindsight serves its own purpose. How many of us can truthfully say that we've always seen God's hand at work in our life? If we're totally honest, the answer will be none of us.

Counseling sessions helped some, but ultimately it was Diane's steadfast belief in Jesus Christ that gave her the clear direction she needed to forge ahead with the rest of her life.

Diane knew she had placed her faith in the only One who could put the puzzle pieces of her life back together again.

While many individuals would remain bitter about the varied circumstances they had to endure, Diane knew she couldn't live her life that way, nor did she want to. She also knew she couldn't halfway give her problems to God. She must completely hand them over to Him and walk away, never looking back. It was only after she fully realized her human frailties, totally surrendered her ongoing problems to God, and stepped aside that she watched God begin to do a mighty work in her life.

Diane has done an impressive job sharing her life story with us. As you read The Rainbow in the Storm (Finding Hope Where There Isn't Any), you will quickly see God's loving, merciful hand at work repeatedly in the life of one of His children. Allow yourself to become immersed in the scriptures and the parts of Diane's life she so willingly shares with us.

Blessings,

Pat Brannon, Christian poet & children's author Author of Walk Softly (You're Steppin' On My Heart!), Filthy Farley O'Charlie McBarley, & Food Fight Frenzy (Thumpin' Through the Third Grade series)

Preface

There are many people, who are hurting, who sit in their "ashes of despair" with no way out, and then there are people who are hurting, and have tried to find a way out, but have become helplessly lost with no hope to cling to. "The Rainbow in the Storm: Finding Hope Where There Isn't Any" will become a tool, with the Bible to help you understand that even though you are experiencing rough storms in your life…there is hope and a way out that will give you a renewed strength, so you, too, can experience the rainbow after the storm.

This book came about through many painful moments in my life. When I was growing up, I never knew that God had this kind of a life planned for me. Now I truly believe that when I was born, God actually branded me for such a moment as this.

God had to bring me to a place where all I could do was look up from my pit of despair, so He could begin the work in me that He had planned since the day I was born. Once

He got my attention and I cried out to Him; He drew me up and out of that pit of despair and began a new work in me.

The reason I've written this book is because God called me to write this book; but also I remember a time when I asked God to break my heart in little pieces for those who suffer as I have and He did.

Throughout many painful moments of counseling and physical pain, God gave me verses and words of encouragement to help me and lift me up and out of my pit of despair. Now, through my own broken heart for others, I desire to share these words with those who are hurting too. I believe that the God that helped me is the same God that can help many.

Introduction

Within these pages, you will read about the painful moments I experienced so God could take my weaknesses and exchange them for His perfect strength.

You will go with me as I go through twenty-one knee surgeries, sexual abuse, the loss of children, and the difficult moments as I came off prescription drugs. You will see how God allowed even more loss in my life so I could gain Him in a greater way.

You will discover how God taught me to rise above my circumstances and you will read how God brought me through some dark and hopeless moments so I could find His light of hope. The book will show you how God allowed each circumstance for a reason, so He could repair my broken vessel and teach me to hear His voice instead of my own.

The first ten chapters of the book tell stories about the most painful moments of my life. Then as you begin to read the middle section of the book, you will read the Bible verses God shared with me while I felt so alone in despair. Each Bible verse that's listed will also explain how God used each verse to draw me closer to Him. Finally, as you approach the end of the book, I've titled my ending "Dear Reader" so we can share together, on a more personal level; so you, too, can find hope, to come out of your own moments of pain and heartache.

Many times we don't fully understand why God allows such suffering. Instead of trying to figure God out, we need to humble ourselves so He can take our circumstances and exchange them for His perfect strength, and then God will be able to use us as mighty vessels for Him.

Table of Contents

Chapter 1
Unknown Pain

I grew up in the small town of Lapeer, Michigan. I was first raised in a small home not far from downtown Lapeer. Around the age of seven or eight we moved into a subdivision on the outskirts of Lapeer. I am the second oldest of four children. As a young girl I loved to run and play and, most of all, I loved to ride my bike. When we moved, we had a pathway that went between my great grandfather's house and ours; we would go and visit my great grandfather and my mom would pick wild asparagus and berries and my two brothers, my sister, and I would stuff our faces with every kind of apple from his orchard.

One day, while I was playing outside at my great grandfather's place, I suddenly fell. I will never forget the pain that went through my knee at that moment. It was like nothing I had ever experienced before. I became frightened because I didn't know what was happening to my knee.

Later, my Mom took me in to see our doctor. She had to carry me in because I couldn't even walk on the leg. It was hard for me, as a young girl, to understand what was happening. After examining my knee, the doctor took x-rays and he told us that my knee had dislocated and the kneecap was still out of place. I watched the doctor as he picked up a reflex hammer. All that was going through my mind, for that moment, was the hammer and what he planned to use it for. I had never seen or experienced anything like this before. I will never forget the feeling as I felt the kneecap ricochet back into place as he tapped on the side of my knee with the reflex hammer. After fixing the knee and reviewing the x-rays once more, our doctor felt that we needed to see an orthopedic specialist.

Our doctor set up an appointment with an orthopedic specialist in Flint, Michigan. I remember the doctor was a big man and it seemed as though his whole hand could wrap around my small leg. After carefully examining my knees and viewing the x-rays, he found out that the grooves in my knee joints weren't holding my kneecap in place as they should. He mentioned that he would have to do surgery to try and correct the problem, but there was only so much he could do because I was still growing. Even though I was young, I thought about the words he had said all the way home. I had never had a surgery before, so I had no idea of what would be ahead for me.

The time finally came for what I thought would be my first and only knee surgery. My orthopedic surgeon from Flint had agreed to do the surgery in Lapeer because this was my first surgery and I was so young. As I walked into the hospital for the first time, I felt as though my whole body was in a state of shock; after all, I was only about ten years old.

After waiting a while for my room to be ready, I was finally taken to where I would spend the night until going into surgery the next morning. That night I had blood drawn and then I was taken to radiology for a chest x-ray. At that time, a patient was admitted the night before so they could do the tests that were needed before surgery.

The next morning, my nurse came in and woke me up and said it was time to get around for surgery. She asked me to take a shower and then they shaved my knee. As I was in the shower, I felt the moments finally arriving that I had thought about for the past weeks.

Later that morning, I was wheeled into pre-op. I started to look around as nurses and doctors were coming from all directions. I remembered a girl who was being wheeled in next to my cart. She was having her tonsils removed. As I looked over to where this young girl was, I saw her crying. I began to feel her pain as each teardrop fell from her cheeks. She was experiencing and feeling the unknown, as I was, as we both were getting ready to enter the operating room for the very first time. Even as I was about to face my very first surgery, I felt the connection between her heart and mine and with that bond I began to comfort her, as if I had known her for a long time.

The nurses continued to line up more patients next to us and as I saw the line of patients begin to grow even more, I began to feel so much fear for what I was about to face. The head nurse came out and began to call out our last names and the operating room we would be in. I began to feel my heart sink for this young girl and myself as the nurses began to wheel each of us, separately, into our own operating room.

As the nurses were wheeling me into the operating room, I remember looking at a tray of instruments to my right and huge lights hanging from the ceiling. I will never forget that moment. All I wanted to do was go to sleep so I wouldn't have to view anymore. I was relieved when I began to see the mask coming over my face. Before I knew it, I felt myself drifting off to sleep.

It seemed like I was only asleep for a moment, then I was awake and in a lot of pain. I had felt pain when my knee dislocated, but this pain was so much more. The nurses noticed that I was awake and they came over and asked me how the pain was and I told them that the pain was really bad, as I was trying to hold back the tears. A nurse gave me a shot of medicine and then the pain began to subside. Within a short time the nurses were wheeling me back to my room.

After the surgery, until I went home, I had a cute, little nurse, who would zip here, there, and everywhere. She would give me sponge baths and rub my feet and make me feel like I had a second mother. In those days, there were no physical therapists so she would help me get up on my crutches. There were days when I would give her trouble because every time I let that bad leg hang over the bed, it felt like the blood in my leg was rushing immediately to the place where my doctor had operated. I got away with not getting out of bed until the nurse had a talk with my parents. After that talk I was getting up and obeying the nurse, even though it hurt so much.

I was in the hospital for about a week or two and then I went home...cast and all. As I began to heal, eventually the cast came off. I remember sitting in a tub of warm water as I tried to bend my knee and get the stiffness out. It felt like I was trying to bend a 2x4 piece of wood. The recovery days seemed long and hard, especially since I knew all the other kids in the neighborhood were outside having fun.

Chapter 2
God Works through Pain

Eventually, the other knee had to be operated on after having more dislocations because both knees had the same problem. As the years passed by, there were many more surgeries. There was really no known cure for my problem, so the doctors just did what they could do to stabilize my knees. Over a period of about thirty-five years, I had a total of twenty-one knee surgeries, and still, to this day, I live with a rod in my right leg and my left leg still remains in poor condition.

I was now into my teen years and God was beginning to work even more, even though I didn't realize it at the time. I was being admitted for another surgery and, as I was taken to my hospital room, I met a lady who had pins in her foot with weights that hung over the end of her bed. She appeared to be a nice lady. She told me that her foot was broken, but that's all she had said. We began to talk even more and, before we realized it, we were becoming good friends. The nurses would push our beds together while we were recovering and we would work on a craft together or just visit and watch TV. Now that I look back, a bond was being formed between a woman and a young girl. We were beginning to feel each other's pain, even though we didn't see it that way at the moment. Neither one of us was able to get out of bed, so when my Mom would come to the hospital to visit with me, she kind of became a second mom to my roommate. She would visit with both of us and she would even wash our hair in bed. At that time, I never knew that being a patient could be so much fun.

It was approaching Valentine's Day and I noticed that my roommate's husband had brought in a box of candy for her but she just laid the box of candy over on the windowsill and completely ignored him. I thought this was strange, but at the same time I felt that she would tell me if something was wrong.

After her husband left, we were watching some TV together and she began to ask me how I was able to cope with all the surgeries I had already gone through. I mentioned to her that I was a Christian and the only reason I was able to endure all this pain was because I had Jesus living in me. After answering her question, I thought it was kind of strange for her to ask me that kind of a question while we were just watching TV together. As we went back to watching TV, all of a sudden, out of nowhere, she began to cry. I couldn't figure out why she would be crying when we were watching just an ordinary TV program. I asked her what was wrong. She told me that she had lied to the doctor and nurses about her injuries and how they had happened. She said that instead of falling on her own, her husband had beaten her and pushed her down the stairs at home. Then she said that her son had sneaked upstairs and crawled under the bed with the phone and had called for help. I asked her why she was telling me all of this and she said that her husband had just called earlier and threatened to kill her the next time he saw her. I began to feel fear and I know that she was already feeling the same feelings as I was.

After she had told me everything, I told her that we should pull the call light so she could tell the nurse what she had told me...She finally agreed and within a short time, a nurse came in our room. My roommate began to break down in tears as she told the nurse that she had been abused by her husband and that he had beaten her and pushed her down the stairs. As she continued, she told the nurse that she had lied about her injuries because she was afraid that her husband might kill her or her son for telling the truth. Before the night was over, there were a couple of nurses in the room, along with her doctor and the police. As the police continued to ask her all kinds of questions, I began to piece everything together in my mind that I had seen before this night. I just sat there, thinking about how I met this lady and how we became friends...thinking she was just an ordinary hospital roommate and then finally I learn about everything she had been through. God was already working, even though I wasn't seeing it His way yet. Before the police left, they told her that they would go and find her husband and make sure her son was safe. As I looked over to my new friend, I began to see a sigh of relief on her face, as she had finally opened up the truth to those around her bed that night.

As the days passed, I continued to share with her about Jesus. Finally, it was time for me to go home. I knew that we would miss each other and it would be hard to say good-bye because we had shared a quick, but special, relationship in that small hospital room. She hadn't accepted Jesus yet but a seed was planted in her heart and mind and she was finally set free from the abuse she had been going through for so long.

Later, a time came when my orthopedic doctor in Flint, Michigan wasn't able to do anything more for my knees. My doctor had done all he could do and still the surgeries weren't helping me. I was still experiencing painful dislocations in both of my knees.

From there, I was referred to another orthopedic specialist in Lansing, Michigan. This specialist had a different technique that he wanted to try, so surgery was scheduled once more. I was admitted to a University hospital and I remember being wheeled into an operating room that had cameras and microphones hanging down. There were also curtains in the operating room and after I was put to sleep, the curtains were opened so students could view my surgery.

The day before surgery, I was given a room with another lady. She was Vietnamese. She had arthritis throughout her whole body and she was admitted for special treatments to help ease the pain. Because my home was a ways from the hospital, I didn't always get a lot of company, so when her children would come to visit her after school, they would visit with me, too. After a few days, her children would bring me pictures that they had colored just for me. When I spent time with her children, I felt like it was God's way of taking care of me while I was so far from home.

The morning of my surgery, my roommate and I began to visit. As she was asking me questions about my knee problems, she started to ask me how I was able to go through so much as a young girl. I mentioned to her that it was because of Jesus. I told her that He was my strength. After we had talked for a while, she turned to me and said, "Can I know Jesus, too?" My heart felt so overwhelmed, but excited. I had my mind made up...no one was going to take me to surgery until my pastor came up. I wanted him to lead this lady to the Lord. It seemed that my roommate's decision to come to Jesus was pushing away my own fears and thoughts of the surgery I was about to face. Within a few moments, my pastor walked into my room. He had come to pray with me before surgery. I was still so excited that I turned to my pastor and said, "I will be fine. Instead, would you lead this lady to Jesus?" What a surprise for him...to walk into my room, thinking that he was just there to pray with me before surgery, and then to find out that he was going to be the one to lead this lady to Jesus.

My pastor didn't have his regular Bible with him, at the time. He just had a smaller testament that he used when visiting and praying for people before surgery, so he asked me if he could borrow mine. I said sure with an overwhelming heart. As I handed my Bible to him, he noticed that my Bible had looked used and he said to me, "I don't normally see many teenagers with a worn Bible." From there, he walked across the room to my roommate's bed and as he sat by her bedside he began to lead her to Jesus. I know that all of Heaven had to be rejoicing!

God had used this surgery to lead this woman to Jesus. God has special reasons why we suffer. I believe that some of the reasons will be made clear to us now and some later. It's all in His good time. We are each a piece of God's puzzle. Some pieces slide right into place but some pieces have a harder time finding their place in the puzzle of life. When each piece is put into its own special place, all the pieces come together and they make something beautiful for God.

The surgeries began to take their toll and I began to lose a lot of special things in my life. I loved to ride my bike downtown with my brother and play tennis and I remember getting pretty good at ice-skating, but most of all I loved my bike. I would have lived on that bike if I could have, but then I remember the day the doctor said, "No more ice-skating, no more tennis, and no more bike riding." It was hard for a girl in her teens to give up all these things. Why was God allowing this to happen to me? I remember many days that I watched the kids my age while they were having fun. My heart was breaking in pieces as I was beginning to feel myself sitting on the sidelines. There were so many days that I felt all alone in my own little world of disabilities.

Chapter 3
From Good to Bad

As I entered my twenties, God was leading me to the man I would marry. In the back of my mind I often wondered if I would even be married at all; after all, who would want to deal with all my pain, surgeries, and scars.

When I met my husband-to-be, I was working as a general office clerk in the hospital in Lapeer, Michigan. Before leaving for work one day, I decided to go and do my laundry at a nearby laundromat. As I was folding my clothes, I noticed a guy and his father. They were doing their laundry, too. I began to laugh as I saw this man trying to teach his Dad how to do laundry. It became comical, like watching an old comedy. As I was laughing to myself, the guy came over to my table and introduced himself to me. When I finished folding my clothes, he offered to carry my laundry out to my car. As we said our good-byes, I began to think about that moment. I thought to myself...too bad I will probably never see that nice guy again.

Later that afternoon, I went to work at the hospital. As I came out to talk to the lady who was passing out visitor cards, guess who came through the front door of the hospital? Yes, it was the guy I had met earlier at the laundromat. Later, I found out that he was coming to the hospital to visit his mother, who was dying of cancer.

Within a short time we began to date. Even on our first date, we seemed to know that we were meant for each other. Within a period of about seven months, we were married and brought together as one with God.

Just after getting married, God led us to Spokane, Washington, where my husband was working. Within about four months of moving to Spokane, I was dealing with a disease called endometriosis that eventually led to a total hysterectomy. This was a very difficult time in my life. At this point I had been through numerous knee surgeries and now I was dealing with a complete hysterectomy. I continued to wonder what God was doing with my life.

I remember the awful days as I was trying to get my hormones balanced. Even though my husband was there for me, I began to feel so alone inside. There were times that I would sit on my bed and cry out to God. My heart felt like it was permanently broken, with no repair in sight. It was bad enough that I had to deal with the knee surgeries, but why God, why did I have to go through this?

Chapter 4
A New Pain

Later, my husband and I had moved into a duplex out in Spokane Valley. One day while my husband was at work, I was watching a movie that dealt with child molestation. For some reason, I was feeling very unusual, as if something had just appeared out of nowhere. The movie had begun to trigger my mind, as I began to remember my own time of molestation. I sat there on the couch in tears. The awful memory had come back, as I began to realize that I had been molested by my Grandfather. I had suppressed the memory for most of my life and suddenly, while I was watching the movie, the memory had appeared before my eyes, just as if I had turned a light switch from off to on.

Many hard days followed as I became suicidal. As each memory flashed before my eyes, like a slide show, I found myself losing control. At the time I was a Christian, but I wasn't spiritually strong enough to face this kind of problem, so I just literally collapsed. I had to be hospitalized so I could receive medication to balance out the fluids in my brain, due to living with depression for so long. I couldn't even make our bed in the morning without crying and falling to the floor. Everything around me began to look dirty, and no matter how many times I cleaned the kitchen, I still felt the need to scrub and clean it even more.

When I first met the doctor who would be working with me, he reached out his hand to me, but I couldn't even shake his hand. I remember him saying, "That's ok, Diane…there will come a day when you will be able to shake my hand." Then he left the room.

While I stayed in the hospital, I received counseling with a nurse that specialized in what I was going through. I remember many days when I thought I would never come home. Christmas was getting closer and all I wanted was to be at home with my husband for Christmas. As Christmas Eve came, I remember pacing the hallways at the hospital, with tears coming down my face, while I felt lost and alone. At that point in my life I didn't know where God was.

On Christmas day, my husband was allowed to bring dinner for the two of us into my room. He had found a restaurant that was open on Christmas day and he mentioned to the manager that he wanted to take some food up to me at the hospital. The manager gave my husband a couple of foam containers and told him to go down the buffet line and get what he wanted. As soon as my husband was done, he went to pay and the manager said there was no charge, and then he said, "Merry Christmas." My husband thanked him as he began to head back up to the hospital. I remember sitting at a small table in my room with my husband as we ate Christmas dinner together.

After finally leaving the hospital, I knew I had a long, hard road ahead of me. There were many moments that I would cry out to God and say, "I don't understand; is this all I was born for; to just keep going through one thing after another? What's next?"

As soon as I came home from the hospital, I was placed in group counseling, along with other women who had gone through molestation. I was nervous and unsettled with the thought of sharing these memories with women I didn't know, so I got this idea that I would memorize a Bible verse and take it with me to counseling. That way, I would have something to balance my thoughts with.

As weeks passed by, I began to feel frustrated because I couldn't talk this over with my Grandfather. He had died years before the memory had surfaced. I was beginning to feel not only the pain of the abuse, but I was also starting to feel as though he had taken the easy way out and had left all of the mixed up feelings behind, with me.

My husband and I had finally decided to plan a trip back home to Michigan. I had felt that maybe I could resolve the problem by going home. As we arrived in Michigan, we had plans to stay with my parents. When we arrived, it was Easter Sunday and my Grandmother had pretty well invited herself over for Easter dinner. As I got out of our van, my Dad came out of the house and ran to tell us that she was there. I knew that I couldn't face her because she was the wife of my abuser, so my husband and I went and got something to eat.

After we were finished, we took a drive out to the cemetery where my Grandfather was buried. I told my husband that I wanted to go alone to his grave, so he waited in our van. As I approached my Grandfather's grave, I began to feel a huge amount of anger swelling within me. I had enough anger in me that when I began to push on my Grandfather's tombstone; I actually was able to move the stone. I remember standing there and asking him why he had done such a thing to me; then I took some mud and crossed out his name on the stone. I thought that after getting all the anger out that I would feel better, but I didn't.

Later, my husband took me to the house I was first raised in. This was the place where my Grandfather had sexually abused me. As we approached the little house that seemed so big to me as a child, I got out of the van and walked to the door. As I began knocking on the door, a real nice lady answered. I explained to her that when I was a child my Grandfather had molested me in this house. I mentioned to her that my husband and I had come all the way from Washington state so I could better deal with the problem. Then I asked her if it would be alright for me to come in and sit for a minute. She told me that a cousin of hers had been going through the same thing and she understood; then she said that I could come in. She let me walk into the living room where the molestation had occurred. As I sat down, I could picture the whole layout of the room as it was when I was a child. I began to relive those awful moments, as I sat there in tears. Somehow I knew God was leading me back here for a reason. I felt as though I was grieving the lost memory from my past. Within a few minutes, the lady came to see if I was alright. I told her that I was alright, and as I began to leave the room, I thanked her for letting me into her house.

As we were approaching the end of our visit, I still was feeling a lot of emotions, so I decided to make one more final trip to the cemetery. I had asked my parents if they would go with us to the cemetery. They agreed to come, but by the next day I had changed my mind. I felt that God wanted me alone with Him, so my husband and I went alone.

As we approached the cemetery for the final visit, I could feel God working with me. He began to show me that I needed to mentally bury all the pain with the one who had hurt me, so I began to do so. As I began to bury every painful moment, I felt like a very heavy load had been taken off my back. For each moment of pain I buried, God began to replace the painful feelings with His peace. From there, I knew that I would have to forgive my Grandfather. If I wanted God to forgive my sins, then I would have to find a way to forgive him, too. I started to feel pity for my Grandfather instead of anger. I knew that one day, he would have to stand before God and be judged for what he had done. As I was sitting on a nearby stump, I began to sing, "I surrender all, I surrender all, all to thee my blessed Savior, I surrender all." As I finished singing, I began to give all the anger and lack of forgiveness over to God, so He could nail all of my feelings to His cross, where once He died to set us free. I began to walk back to the van, and as I left the cemetery I cried because I had finally been set free.

Chapter 5
More Surgeries

After returning home, I began to have more problems with my right knee. How could I go through one more thing in my life? I began to wonder why I was being hit with one problem after another. I was beginning to feel that I was going through more problems than I could handle. Why was God allowing so much suffering in my life?

We were still living in the duplex and there were two sets of stairs; one of the sets of stairs led up to a bathroom and two bedrooms and the stairs leading down went to a family room, another bedroom and a half bath/laundry room.

One day, I was coming down the stairs from our bedroom to our living room and my knee dislocated. Because I was on the stairs at the time, I flew through the air and landed on the floor. The pain was excruciating and my body began to shake from the pain. When I went to turn over, I thought that I had somehow broke my knee joint because there was a bone laying way over to the right side of my knee. I began to panic! The pain continued to overwhelm me. I called out to my husband and he came running down the stairs. When he saw my knee, he immediately reached down and grabbed on to the bone, which was my kneecap and pulled it to the center of my knee. I had never experienced anything like that, ever! It was amazing, how God gave my husband the strength to do what he did! My knee began to instantly swell, as I felt my body going into shock from the pain. My husband took me up to the emergency room and they gave me a shot for the pain and placed ice on my melon shaped knee and told me to follow up with my doctor.

Later in the week, my husband took me to my orthopedic surgeon and the doctor set me up for another surgery to try and stabilize the knee. I began to feel like, "Here we go again...will there ever be an end to all of this pain?" I just sat in his office and began to weep, as my husband consoled me.

When I was in surgery, the doctor noticed that my tendon had ruptured, probably during the fall, so he repaired the tendon with a donor tendon. This surgery started to become like all the other surgeries. I would go into the operating room and come out in more pain than when I first entered. The surgeries were becoming so old that I felt like vomiting when I would begin to think of them.

I will never forget the long weeks ahead as I returned home from the hospital. I remained in my bedroom for about three months because the only main bathroom was upstairs. I couldn't take a chance on the other knee dislocating, so I only came downstairs for my doctor appointments.

My sister had come out for a visit, not too long after I had been released from the hospital, to give my husband a break, as he had to return back to work. His employer had given him some time off so he could be at the hospital and help me when I first came home. My sister's visit helped me, at first, to tolerate being upstairs all the time. When my husband was at work I had someone to visit with, but when she left it seemed like depression was trying to creep in and take control of me. So, now, I was not only dealing with the post-op pain, but I was also dealing with depression and loneliness.

As I remained upstairs the hours went very slow. My husband had already taken off as much time as he was able to, so I was once more alone. There were days that I cried as I saw my neighbors going out every day. I began to feel alone again in my disability. Days would go by with no phone calls or visits. I started to become angry! I couldn't figure out what God was doing. Why was God allowing me to feel so alone and depressed while being in pain, too?

A time came when the doctor said, "No more stairs." As I began to heal from the previous surgery, I wanted to stay at this place so badly but I knew in my heart that I couldn't handle the stairs. I couldn't take another chance that one of my knees might dislocate again. Maybe the next time would be worse.

Just before the move, I was having more pain in the right knee and I noticed that the kneecap was more off to the left side of my knee. I had just changed to a different orthopaedic doctor, so I set up an appointment to have him check my knee. After taking x-rays, the doctor felt that the kneecap wasn't positioned right. He felt that the kneecap needed to be fixed, so I was scheduled for surgery once more. As each surgery continued to come, I felt as though I was becoming numb in some way. The tears that once flowed so hard down my cheeks became closed within my heart as my heart began to cry out to God.

My husband and I were finally able to find a place to stay with no stairs and within a short time from moving I had surgery and the problem was repaired. This recovery didn't seem to be as depressing at the beginning because we lived in a one story duplex. Instead of the crutches, I was able to use a walker. I had made a bag out of fabric that I could hook to my walker and I would carry everything in that bag as I walked through the house. I even carried my lunch and the dog goodies in that bag I made, while my husband worked at night. My dogs had only seen me on a walker, crutches, or cane, so they made my life easier, too. When I would walk, they would walk behind me and when I stopped, they would stop, too. In fact, my husband would go to work and say, "Take care of Mommy," and you know, they did. One evening, while my husband was gone to work, I was in the bathroom and I guess that my dog had thought I was in there too long so she pushed the door open with her head, as though to say, "Are you ok?" I told her that Mommy was ok and she went back out in the hallway and waited until I came out.

After the previous surgery, I went in for outpatient surgery so my doctor could clean out all the scar tissue that had formed from previous injuries and surgeries. So there were many more recovery days to come. The surgeries continued to take a toll with me and my body and by this time I didn't know what to think. At times, I wondered if this was going to become my life till the day I died.

Chapter 6
Hope for a New Start

When I was younger, my orthopedic surgeon had told my Mom and me that later I might have to have both knees replaced. As I was thinking about that, I decided to set up an appointment with my current orthopedic surgeon because I was still having some pain and difficulties with my right knee.

The appointment day finally came. My husband and I talked with my doctor and I asked him if he would consider doing a joint replacement surgery because I was having a hard time with the pain in the right knee. After talking with the doctor, he finally agreed to do the joint replacement on my right knee. I began to feel that this surgery would finally be the last operation.

I remember being wheeled into the operating room for the eighteenth time. I could see all the instruments around me. The nurses were busy preparing the room for my new joint replacement. I knew that God was with me, as I felt His presence by the operating table. I still couldn't figure out what

God was doing in my life. All I knew was that the surgeries were getting very old!

After coming out of surgery, I had a lot of hard work ahead of me. A physical therapist was brought into our home until I was able to go to therapy. When I was able to go to therapy, my doctor scheduled me for regular therapy and pool therapy. The hardest part was working with the stiffness in the new knee joint and trying to increase the strength back into my leg. The therapy was difficult, but I was determined to get through the moments so I could enjoy my new joint.

Chapter 7
A Long Road Ahead

One day, as I was doing my pool therapy, I noticed that my scar looked red and I was experiencing more pain at times. I just figured that this was happening from being in the pool and exercising the knee.

A few days later, I was working on a project in our bedroom, when I noticed that my knee looked splotchy. I was also beginning to feel as if I was running a fever, so I sat down and took my temperature and it was near 100 degrees. I called the doctor and as I was telling the lady over the phone about my knee and what was happening, she told me that the doctor should take a look at my knee, so she set up an appointment for me that day.

By time I got there, the splotches were still there and my temperature was 100.5. The doctor decided to admit me to the hospital. He told us that there might be infection in the new joint. He said that there was a chance that the new joint might have to be removed. I began to cry out loud because the one true chance I had was slipping through my fingers.

Over the next couple of days, the doctor kept a close watch and took fluid samples out of my knee. All I could think about was, "What's next, God?" I couldn't figure out why God was allowing one thing to keep happening after another. I began to question why I was born. After all, there was no purpose to my life. What purpose would all these surgeries serve? I felt blinded by what I was experiencing. I was still walking down God's pathway but my vision was being fogged over by my overwhelming circumstance.

Within a couple days, my fever went down and the splotches began to go away, so my doctor sent me home. He wanted me to set up a follow up appointment, so I did.

Within a short time, my husband and I were back in the doctor's office. We sat down together and talked with the doctor and he thought that we shouldn't take any risks in case there was some infection. He felt that the new joint should be removed. My husband and I began to see that we couldn't take a chance, in case the infection was there, so we had his office schedule me for surgery. We had to wait a few days to a week, while all the arrangements were being made.

As we left the doctor's office, all that kept going through my mind were the words that the doctor had spoken to us. He told us that the new knee joint would have to be removed, and then he would place a small box in my knee that would be filled with a time released antibiotic that would stay in my knee for six weeks. He mentioned to me that I would have an IV line put into my arm before going home, so antibiotics could be administered every so many hours. Then he mentioned that after six weeks, I would come back to the hospital for a second surgery to put in another new knee joint.

As I went home from my appointment, my head was so overwhelmed with all the information that I completely fell apart. I remember calling my mom and sobbing out of control on the phone. I mentioned to her that I would have to go through two major surgeries within six weeks time. I didn't know how these surgeries were going to work out with my husband's job. My mom told me that she would fly out after the second surgery so my husband could return to work. After talking with my Mom for a while, I began to see a glimpse of light breaking through what seemed to be a very dark moment in my life.

Finally, the day for the first surgery had arrived. I was so nervous because even though I had been through other surgeries, I knew that these two surgeries would be different.

As the nurses wheeled me into the operating room, I was placed on the operating table, and before I knew it, I was fast asleep. It seemed that I had just fallen asleep and then I was awake again. After coming out of recovery, I was put into an isolation room due to the possible infection.

After a day or two, I started to think on all that was ahead of me and I started to cry. I thought, "Oh God, I can't do this!" A nurse heard me crying while she was passing by my room and she came in and asked me if I was all right. I told her why I was crying, and I will never forget that moment. She placed her arms around me and gave me a big hug and said that everything would be all right. After I had settled down, from that moment on, she would come in my room once in awhile to check on me and make sure I was all right. That moment felt like God had heard my cry and came down and held me in His mighty arms of love.

Before I went home, an IV line was placed into my arm and when I got home from the hospital, a nurse came over and showed us how to administer the antibiotics. She also came to our home and changed the dressing around the IV line and then she checked my vitals. My husband would insert the large syringe into the IV line and then he would give me the antibiotics. There were nights that we would have to set the alarm so he could give me antibiotics during the night.

One evening I noticed that the site around the IV line looked discolored, so we called the nurse. She said that we should go up to the emergency room and have the IV line checked out. I was still hurting from the surgery and I remember the weather was cold and snowy but the nurse told us that it was important, so my husband helped me get ready to go.

As we arrived at the emergency room, I remember sitting in a wheelchair while we waited for the doctor to check the IV line. I was so tired and I was in a lot of pain. All I wanted to do was go home. Finally, the doctor walked in and checked my IV line. He said that the site appeared to be infected and the IV line would have to be taken out and replaced with a new one. I was taken to an empty room and the old IV line was removed, then the site was thoroughly cleaned and a new IV line was inserted again into my arm. After what seemed to be forever, I was finally able to go home and rest.

The nurse continued to come to our home and check the IV line and change the dressings. From there, the days passed by until the six weeks were coming to an end. After having the first surgery behind me, an automatic appointment had been in place for the final surgery. All I wanted was to get this surgery over with and put all of this behind me.

As I was being wheeled into surgery, all I could think of was, "Here we go again!" Within a minute or two, I was fast asleep as my surgeon prepared to put in a brand new joint. It seemed as if it was only minutes and then I began to wake up in recovery. The surgical pain became very real, but as I returned to my room, I gradually came back to reality and I began to feel that all of the surgeries had finally come to an end; at least that's what I thought.

As I began to slowly recover, my doctor placed me back into regular physical therapy and pool therapy. I always looked forward to the pool therapy because the warm water made my knee feel better. Most of the regular therapy was being used to strengthen the muscles and to get the stiffness out of the knee. Many times the therapist would have me dangle my leg over the edge of the table, and then he would push in on the lower leg so he could get the knee to bend. Oh, how painful that was! I dreaded every time the therapist would work on my knee. I continued in physical therapy until the therapists had done all they could do. I was hoping and praying that the new joint would begin to work now and the pain would eventually leave.

Chapter 8
Why, God?

Time continued to pass by, but the pain and warmth on the right side of my new joint wasn't going away. I became so discouraged and I couldn't understand why God would bring me out of the infection to more pain.

I continued to see my orthopedic surgeon, but when I'd go in for the appointments, I would come out the same way with no answers. The moments of despair kept piling up on each other as hope for me became like a window that remained permanently shut.

At an earlier appointment my doctor suggested that maybe I should have the knee joint fused. That would mean taking the joint out and replacing the joint with a rod. When I first discussed this idea with him, I broke down into tears. How was I supposed to go through another surgery, especially one like this? It seemed that God's pathway for me was being filled with more rocks, which became harder to climb over. I went home and all I could do was cry out to God. I never really knew what to say to God by that time. I felt so empty, with no words left to speak. I felt like the problem with my knees had become an old movie that I had continually watched, over and over again.

As the weeks passed by, the doctor told me that I could either make the decision to have the fusion or he told me that he would help me make the decision. I began to balance my thoughts as I talked with God, but by this point I couldn't feel anything because I was already totally drained from all that I had already been through. How was I to know what God wanted if I was so clouded over by the circumstance I was facing? At moments, I felt like this decision had become like a thick fog. I knew that God was there but I just couldn't find Him at times.

As I began to think about the surgery more, I felt that I would end up hurting the rest of my life if I didn't do something, so I finally agreed to have the surgery. I felt that anything would be better than this pain I was living with. Although I made this decision, later I felt that I hadn't given God enough time to show me the true way. I felt that I was looking at the problem through my own eyes instead of God's. As I look back to those moments, I feel that I had just given up because I was just too drained emotionally. I had let my decision become greater than God, and while my decision became too hard to deal with, I was making God weaker in my life without realizing what I was doing.

Surgery was scheduled and before I knew it, the day had arrived. At this point my body was so tired from all the previous surgeries that I began to wonder if I would make it through this surgery. As I was being wheeled into the operating room, I saw a whole table filled with metal tools that would be used during surgery. I felt like I was entering a metal shop. After seeing the tools I began to wonder if I had made the right decision.

After viewing the room, I was laid on the operating table and put to sleep. Later that evening, after surgery, I was told that my doctor had a hard time removing the artificial joint due to the calcification that had already formed around the joint. He had to hammer the joint out, and because of that, there was bone damage that made my right leg about a quarter of an inch shorter then my left leg. What a surprise when I got up on my leg for the first time! I felt like I was lopsided and I found it difficult to maintain my balance. I just remember looking at my husband, with tears flowing down my face, as I thought, what is happening to me?

After surgery, I really gave no thought to how my leg would feel, to never bend it again. The physical therapists worked on leg strengthening but that was all the therapy I received. In the past, the therapists would come into my room and they would be already trying to get the knee to bend but not this time. At the moment, I remember the good feelings I had because I wasn't going to have to go through the painful kind of therapy that I had endured in the past.

Finally, the day came when the brace and bandages would be removed, along with the stitches too. As I returned home from my appointment, I felt as though I was waking up to reality. My heart sank within me, as I began to think about all the things I would no longer be able to do. I wouldn't be able to sit in a chair without having to have a footstool around to support my leg. There would be no more kneeling to pray either. As many more thoughts began to cross my mind, a piece of my heart began to break for all the things I would no longer be able to do. For the next few days, I felt like I was mourning the loss of my knee. There were moments when I wanted to try and bend my knee, instead of living with the reality that was creeping into my life. I continually cried out to God until I felt I had shed every tear that I could cry and when the tears began to dry up, I felt as though my heart took over and began to weep. I could see tears falling from the depths of my heart as my heart cried out to God, "Why me?"

Chapter 9
Finding God through Weakness

After the fusion had healed, I still felt pain. There was nothing more that the doctor could do, so an appointment was set up for me at the pain clinic. I was told that my pain could be from all the surgeries and problems I've had with my knees, along with scar tissue.

During the appointment at the pain clinic, a doctor and a nurse practitioner began to interview me. I felt like I had been asked every question that could be asked. It seemed that within moments they had me on five prescriptions and most of them were narcotic medications. I asked the doctor if they either had a natural medication that could be used for my pain or something that was non-narcotic. The doctor mentioned that a non-narcotic medication was being worked on, for chronic pain, but the medication wasn't in the pharmacies yet. I started to feel discouraged again and I felt like nothing was going right. Would my life be like this forever? I was still turning to God, but the rope I was holding on to was getting thinner and thinner. I felt like I was hanging onto the very bottom of a small rope.

As I continued with my appointment, I could tell that the nurse practitioner really cared! She wasn't trying to push anything on me, but she began to show me that my body wouldn't be able to get through this kind of pain, which was mainly bone pain, without a medication to help me each day, so I finally agreed to give their methods a try.

The nurse practitioner had me set up appointments to see her every couple of weeks to start out with so she and the doctor could monitor the medications and my vitals. She would come into the examination room during my appointments and visit with me and then she would report to the doctor. After she had finished talking with the doctor, she would come back into my room to let me know what he wanted to do.

As time passed by, I came to a point that the medications weren't working as well, so the doctor kept increasing the amounts. After increasing the medications, I would feel relief but when my body became immune to the medications, the pain slowly crept back in. At this point I became more and more discouraged. I felt like I was climbing a ladder and never getting anywhere. As I became more discouraged, I began to fall into a depression. I felt like all my past circumstances, along with my current ones, were gradually digging a pit and I was at the bottom...looking up. I just could not understand why God kept allowing one thing after another to happen.

When my pain clinic appointments came, I would talk with the nurse practitioner and tell her that I wanted to come off all the drugs but then she kept showing me that I couldn't live with that kind of pain each day. At this point, I felt like either the drugs were going to kill me or the pain. I would go home discouraged, as I felt myself digging a deeper pit with each discouraging moment. Seems like all my life consisted of was either surgeries or pain. I couldn't face the pit I was in anymore, so I began to search, with all I had left within me, to be free so I could come out of my "pit of despair" and find what God truly desired for my life. How could this be His desire forever?

One day I was trying to relax and watch TV. As I was watching a program, I heard that aloe vera juice was good for joint pain. So I got on my computer and did a little research. As I began to read more and more, I started to see a glimpse of light entering my dark pit of despair. I began to share this information with my husband and he started to get encouraged too.

I began to search through the phone book and I was able to find someone who sold aloe vera juice, so my husband and I set up a time so we could talk with them. After arriving, we sat down and talked with the couple. The more we talked, the more I became excited. I was beginning to feel that God had heard my desperate cry and this was His way of helping me. My husband and I decided to give the aloe vera juice a try, so we bought a couple small jugs and brought them home.

Later that day, I got the juice out of the fridge and started to drink some. The lady we bought the juice from had told us to start slow and then work gradually with the juice. Even though I was still on my medications, I began to feel the edge of my pain leave me as I drank more of the juice. My next pain clinic appointment was getting closer and I was getting excited to tell my nurse practitioner about what I was doing.

My appointment finally arrived and I began to tell my nurse practitioner about the aloe vera juice. I mentioned to her that I wanted to continue the aloe vera juice and try to come off all my medications. I told her that I wanted to see how the aloe vera juice would help my pain. After talking with her, she agreed to help me. I asked her if there was a hospital that they could admit me to so I could come off the medications easier. Some of the medications I was on were considered "big guns," or very strong drugs. She mentioned that there was no place in my area. She also said that she didn't want me to come off the drugs too fast. She stated that if I came off the drugs too fast, then maybe my body would go into shock. So instead, she put me on a plan to wean me off the drugs. I have to admit, I was scared at first, but as I started to think about all the painful moments that God had brought me through, I began to feel that He would help me over these rocks in my pathway.

I went home with a plan to slowly go off one medication at a time. The weeks became hard and difficult, but at the same time I began to truly lean on God and know that He wouldn't let me down.

As I came off one drug, I began to feel hope so I could come off the next one. As I came closer to coming off the last two drugs, I became weaker to the point I could only get up to take a quick shower or use the bathroom and even those simple tasks became like hard chores. I could feel the drugs bringing me from an extreme high to an extreme low. My eyes became blurred and I began to feel chilled and achy. As I gazed at the portrait of Jesus, which was hanging over our fireplace, He would appear pale and blurred. The only way I knew I was getting better was when I looked at the portrait of Jesus and I could see the color coming back in His face.

The nurse practitioner had made a plan so I would be off the drugs within eight weeks, but as I came off the drugs I decided to just finish them, except for the last minor one because I felt that I still needed to take that one with the aloe vera juice. As I worked harder to get off the drugs, I began to lean on God more and more and within four weeks I was off all the drugs except for the last one.

As I returned to my next appointment with the nurse practitioner, she was so surprised to hear how far I had come. The only thing she could say was that it was a miracle. She said that she had never seen anyone come off that many major drugs in that short of a time. My husband and I mentioned to her that we were Christians and that God had helped me. She just stood there in amazement. This was actually the first time that we were able to experience God's special touch in such an awesome way. Through this experience, God taught me to stay focused on Him and His strength instead of the weakness. I feel that this moment was bringing forth a new dawn in my life.

After a period of time, I felt that it was time to go off the final medication. I wanted to see if the aloe vera juice could handle all of my pain. Within a week's time, I was finally off the last medication and I was beginning to increase the aloe vera juice. I was finally able to stop using a cane and make a new start.

For a period of about two years or so I was nearly pain free and then I had to go back on the last minor medication because my left knee had progressively become worse and my right leg, with the rod, had increased with pain.

God was beginning to teach me that if my focus is on Him instead of myself, I will be drawn to walk in His footsteps. Sometimes we are broken down, so all we have to turn to is

Jesus, but when we cry out to Him He will listen and mend what's been broken. One thing God did during the painful years of my life was He allowed me to go down to a state of brokenness so He could bring me back up and teach me to depend on Him more.

Even now, as I write this book, I realize that God used the aloe vera juice to bring back the faith that had been buried and forgotten, for so long, due to the surgeries, pain, and heartache that I went through for so many years of my life. Maybe the aloe vera juice worked to some extent, but even now, I see that it was faith that awakened me and had allowed me to see the rainbow instead of the stormy clouds that had haunted me for so many years of my life.

Chapter 10
Suffering for a Reason

God has already begun to use the painful moments from my past to reach out to others who hurt in a similar way. II Corinthians 12:7-10 has become my life verses: "And less I should be exalted above measure through the abundance of the revelations, there was given to me a thorn in the flesh, the messenger of Satan to buffet me, lest I should be exalted above measure. For this thing I besought the Lord thrice, that it might depart from me. And he said unto me, my grace is sufficient for thee: for my strength is made perfect in weakness. Most gladly therefore will I rather glory in my infirmities, that the power of Christ may rest upon me. Therefore I take pleasure in infirmities, in reproaches, in necessities, in persecutions, in distresses for Christ's sake, for when I am weak, then am I strong."

These Bible verses have taught me that sometimes God has to allow weakness into our life, so we can be humbled down to His level, and then our weaknesses can eventually be used for Him in a stronger way. I realize now that God had to allow all the moments of weakness into my life so I could be at a level with Christ, to hear His voice instead of mine.

Sometimes the moments of weakness can be used for such a long period of time that we begin to wonder if God still loves us. One thing I know, if God doesn't remove the "thorn" of weakness right away, then He will show His love to us as He sustains us. He will hold our hand and walk us through the rocky pathway of circumstance until He's ready to free us of the "thorn." When we understand God's promises, then a peace comes into ourselves that gives us a reason to rejoice.

What an honor and privilege it is to suffer for the cause of Christ. When His power is resting upon us, then others will see Him through us as we rise above our weaknesses and find His strength.

During the many years of surgeries and pain, God took the empty moments of my life and used them in a very awesome and powerful way. Throughout the years of 2002 and 2003, I began to feel like God was very distant in my life, so one day I asked God to fill me with something special so I would be able to feel His presence in a closer way. Within a short time, God began to fill my mind with beautiful words of wisdom that He used to eventually restore my broken spirit. My mind could hardly contain all the words of wisdom that He was giving me.

God was now beginning to communicate with me in a way I had never known before. We were now beginning to walk as one, out of my wilderness of despair, so He could begin to show me the reason for the "thorn." Even though the "thorn" has been with me for so many years of my life, He has shown me that He was always with me, even when I was so overwhelmed with my circumstances and I couldn't feel

His presence. When I was lost in my wilderness of despair He still remained there as He became my sunlight by day and my moonlight by night.

He sought me out with a heart of true love and He gave me His perfect strength and now His power rests upon me. I had to walk out of my wilderness of despair with a renewed strength so I could experience His power in my life. Once I became as one with Him, I then had the strength to climb the mountain with God and even now, as I look down over the deep wilderness of despair that I once traveled…I can see the distance He's brought me and those moments give me strength for what may lie ahead.

God used many Bible verses to keep me strengthened through the painful moments of my life. I can say without a doubt that if God wouldn't have been there for me, teaching me, strengthening me, uplifting me, and, most of all, loving me, then I know that I would be like a ship that's lost at sea. The verses and words that God had given me had become a lifeline to hold tight to, until the storms of my life finally came to an end.

From what I have seen and heard there are many people that need a lifeline to keep them from drowning in their circumstance. When I began this book, I felt God prompting me to share the Bible verses that He had used to help me in my own life. The pages ahead aren't just Bible verses that I copied into the book. I have also shared what God taught me as He used each verse to become a lifeline for my life.

I thank God for the love He gave me and the shelter He provided during the many difficult storms of my life. I pray that each word you read will become a lifeline to you as you are going through the raging storms in your own life. You may feel that the circumstances are making you feel helplessly lost, with no hope in sight. God and I want to give you a brand new hope that will become a lifeline for you to hold to as you gradually exchange your weaknesses for His perfect strength.

Needless Despair

"If ye continue in my word, then are ye my disciples indeed; and he shall know the truth, and the truth shall make you free." —John 8:31b-32

Many times I went through hours of needless despair because I leaned on my circumstance or problem instead of leaning on God's strength and truth.

We, as people, make our lives more difficult than what God has intended for us. Jesus died on the cross so He could keep us free from evil, but instead we get caught up in Satan's deceptive lies and then his lies keep us in bondage. It's only God's truth that breaks the shackles so we can become free.

When you know the truth behind your problems or circumstance but those around you walk away with disbelief, then turn to the God who already knows. He will have the key that will unlock the shackles you've carried for so long and He will set you free forever.

Leaning in the Right Direction

"Trust in the Lord with all thine heart; and lean not unto thine own understanding. In all thy ways acknowledge him, and he shall direct thy paths." –Proverbs 3:5-6

Many times we fail in life because we are leaning on the wrong person. Instead of leaning on our own thoughts and ways, we should lean on God to help us. How is it that we seem to know what God wants when we are just mere men? God is the One who made us so He is the only one who knows how to fix the problems in our lives.

When I got stubborn and I tried to fix the circumstance on my own, it was as if God was standing with His arms folded, looking down from Heaven and saying, "Alright, if you know how to fix your problem then I will just stand back and let you go ahead and try."

As I proceeded to fix the problem my way I began to fall and the first words that came out of my mouth were, "Please God, help me"!

I learned that when I leaned on God instead of myself, I found a greater understanding and a greater wisdom as He began once more to direct my life and put me back on His pathway.

One Way to Heaven

"Thou, which has shewed me great and sore troubles, shalt quicken me again, and shalt bring me up again from the depths of the earth." – Psalm 71:20

When I think of this verse, I visualize a staircase leading up to Heaven. Each step resembles the trials we go through here on earth.

As we learn what God wants us to know, we are being given the strength through Him to climb to the next step.

After going through many trials (steps) in our lives we can begin to feel overwhelmed. If we could just look behind us and see the trials we have overcome through Jesus, then the past moments of victory in our lives would give us hope for what may be ahead of us.

There are times that we may feel that we are always stuck on the same step, but God will always be there to lift us up to the next step and each new step we take will be rewarded with a greater strength.

The Prince of All Peace

"Peace I leave with you, my peace I give unto you; not as the world giveth, give I unto you. Let not your heart be troubled, neither let it be afraid." —John 14:27

One day I was thinking about the word "peace." I've heard people say, "Pray for peace." Can we pray for peace or is peace something that we seek as we walk daily with God?

God showed me that if we have Him living in our hearts and we truly know and love Him, in a personal way, then His peace will always be there for us as an extra benefit or gift from Him.

The peace that we receive from this world is a fragile peace. It's a peace that only stays for a few moments but when you have the peace, which comes along with God's love, then you can go through any obstacle in your life and still feel the comforting peace that can only come from the true God.

Growing Through Affliction

"Before I was afflicted I went astray; but now have I kept thy word. It is good for me that I have been afflicted; that I might learn thy statutes." —Psalm 119:67-71

As I went through many afflictions in my life, sometimes I would wonder why God allowed so many. Then I began to learn that God was allowing the painful moments in my life so He could make me stronger.

First of all, God isn't the one who places afflictions on us, because God is good and good cannot produce evil. Sometimes I find that God will allow affliction to come into our life so He can use our affliction to bring us closer to Him.

Second, it's Satan who attempts to use our afflictions to either destroy us or to take us away from God.

I believe that God takes His authority and sets up boundaries for our lives. He only allows Satan to go so far. Satan thinks that he is going to win but God takes the affliction that Satan put upon us and He turns around and uses the affliction to take us from a point of weakness to His perfect strength. Once God has accomplished His plan with the affliction and we have learned what God wants us to know, God removes the affliction from us.

Rejoicing through Affliction

"Why are thou cast down, O my soul? And why art thou disquieted within me? Hope thou in God; for I shall yet praise him, who is the health of my countenance, and my God." –Psalm 42:11

When we go through painful moments in our lives we tend to get so caught up or distracted with the circumstances we are facing. A lot of the time we don't even realize what we are doing. God taught me to keep my attention fully on Him, along with the things that are of good report; that way I don't have to be concerned about the distractions Satan tries to throw my way because evil cannot thrive where God resides.

One time I asked God, "How do I praise you and rejoice when I'm in so much pain?" He spoke to my heart and said, "Diane, you rejoice because, even though you are hurting, I am here to help you and I am here to strengthen you and, most of all, I have chosen you to suffer so I can be seen through others who suffer too!" God showed me that He's always there; all we need to do is rise above our hurt and seek the one who can help us!

Fixed on God

"He shall not be afraid of evil tidings; his heart is fixed, trusting in the Lord, His heart is established, he shall not be afraid, until he sees his desire upon his enemies." –Psalm 112:7-8

As long as I remained close to God, I didn't have to fear or dread anything in my life. I have finally found a great peace in my life because God's presence has become very real to me.

When I am faced with pain, I have a settled feeling now, because God must have some reason for my pain. If He doesn't remove my pain altogether, I don't fear or dread anything worse because I know that He's in charge and that He's always here to hold my hand and gently help me through.

I look at my life as a long journey and the journey will eventually end in Heaven. With the hope of Heaven in sight, those painful moments just remind me that I'm one more moment closer to my destination.

Focused on God

"Thou wilt keep him in perfect peace, whose mind is stayed on thee: because he trusteth in thee. Trust in the Lord for ever: for in the Lord Jehovah is everlasting strength." –Isaiah 26:3-4

I have found that I don't always have the perfect peace that comes from God, and it's because I take my eyes off Him and then I let my mind sit in "Ashes of Despair." This reminds me of Peter in the Bible. He was walking on the water to Jesus, but when he looked down on the stormy sea, he fell.

When we are facing a raging storm in our life, all we have to do is focus on the one true God who has the power to calm the storms in our lives.

We tend to go through more in our lives than what we need to go through and that's because we put ourselves at a level where only Satan can work, and that's our weakness. All we have to do is talk to God and read His word and draw closer to Him; then we can use the tools He's given us. When we keep our eyes focused on Him then the storms in our lives will begin to cease, and we will find ourselves being rescued as God lifts us up into the safety of His loving arms.

My Helper

"The Lord is my helper, and I will not fear what man shall do unto me." —Hebrews 13:6b

God covers us with Himself to protect us from the hurts of this world. He becomes our helper as we seek Him. We don't have to fear anything because His love will become a shield to defend us from everything that comes our way.

There are many circumstances that we may endure in this life, but God is the same God in all of them. As we call upon His name, He draws closer and closer to us, like a magnet, and He won't let go unless we tell Him to. When we read His word, pray, or just talk with Him on a personal level, we are allowing His presence to surround us.

When we are facing difficult trials and Satan attempts to destroy us with these trials, they bounce off of a protective layer, which is Jesus Christ, and the fiery dart or trial that was meant to destroy us goes back to Satan.

God taught me that it's so important to get close to Him and remain close to Him. We may experience fear through our trials, but remember that there is a God reaching out to you today. He wants to replace those fears with His love!

Cradled in His Loving Arms

"I will both lay me down in peace, and sleep; for thou, Lord, only makest me dwell in safety." –Psalm 4:8

God is an "everything" God. He is a God that is there during the holidays. His work hours are 24 hours a day and 7 days a week. He doesn't even take a break. When we talk to Him, there is no cost for long distance. What a friend to have!

When I was going through my surgeries and I had some nights of pain and restlessness, He taught me how to get back to sleep. All I had to do was get comfortable with my pillow and picture Him, cradling me in His arms of love. As He cradled me, He would keep reminding me that I wasn't alone and that I was in the safety of His arms. In no time, I was falling back to sleep. While He was with me, He was letting me know that He was in charge.

Always There

"For the mountains shall depart and the hills be removed; but my kindness shall not depart from thee, neither shall the covenant of my peace be removed, saith the Lord that hath mercy on thee." –Isaiah 54:10

This verse has been of great strength to me, especially during the hard and difficult moments of my life.

People who live with disabilities, like me, continually face the thought of losing their friends; but this verse is a constant reminder that God will always be there for us. In His word, He has made a vow to you and me that He would never leave us, nor forsake us. He has made a covenant to us that no matter what happens or no matter who walks out of our lives, He will always be there for us.

He is a God that truly knows about each hurt and lonely feeling because He also was ridiculed and persecuted as He died on the cross for our sins.

The world may make promises to you and me and then turn around and break their promises, but God is a God of

His word. He keeps His word to us because He truly understands that kind of hurt.

It was hard for God to let go, as He saw His son die on the cross but when His Father knew what the outcome would be in the end, there was a moment of satisfaction.

We find it hard to suffer, and God our Father finds it hard to see us suffer, but in the end we begin to see the good that comes from it all, then we become satisfied and we begin to rejoice.

Comfort During the Storms

"I will not leave you comfortless; I will come to you." —John 14:18

When I would begin to think of each storm in my life, I would feel despair. As each tall wave of circumstance hit me head on, I began to feel hopeless. All I wanted was for someone to come and rescue me.

I cried out to God and He came to my rescue. He held my hand so I wouldn't have to face the worst of the storm alone. He filled my thoughts with words of comfort and hope.

Through the painful moments, I found God to be a friend that I could lean on. I didn't have to suffer alone because, as God was drawing me closer to Him, I knew that He would always be there. God will stand with you, too, during the worst storms of your life. He will ride the fiercest waves with you and He won't let you go, and after the storm has subsided He will walk with you, until He leads you safely to shore.

The Problem Fixer

"Cast thy burden upon the Lord, and he shall sustain thee: he shall never suffer the righteous to be moved." –Psalm 55:22

God is the only God! He is the one who made you and me and, since He's the one who made us, He's the only one that knows how to fix us and our problems.

If you bought a product and something was wrong with your product, you wouldn't take your product to just any manufacturer to be fixed. No, you would take your product back to the manufacturer who made the product, because they would be the only one who would know how to repair the product.

Since God is the one who made us, then He's the only one who knows how to repair every broken part. When we hurt and there's no way for us to fix the hurt, then we need to go to the one who knows how to fix a hurting mind and a broken heart, and that's God.

There are times that we try to bare our problems on our own shoulders, until we realize that each problem has become a brick of circumstance. As more problems arise, the bricks of circumstance eventually make our own prison wall, and then, later, we find it harder because we have to bring each brick of circumstance down, one brick at a time.

Why not give your circumstances to God at the beginning of the problem so later you don't have to suffer needlessly.

Tried through Fire

"That the trial of your faith, being much more precious than of gold that perisheth, though it be tried with fire, might be found unto praise and honor and glory at the appearing of Jesus Christ." –I Peter 1:7

As I went from one surgery into another, I began to wonder if this was all my life was going to consist of. Why would God allow me to be born, just so I could go from one problem into another?

Little did I know that God had a plan, and in order to fulfill His plan, I would have to go through the storm in order to find the rainbow in my life. In other words, God was taking me through basic training so I could find His heart instead of my own.

As I continued to learn and grow, I realized that God was remolding me His way instead of my way. God wanted me to empty all of Diane out so God could have room to work and be seen in me.

Often I think of it this way; as I begin to walk through a wilderness of trials, God becomes my sun by day and my moonlight by night. He is allowing me to stay out in the wilderness until I begin to lean on Him instead of myself. As I continue to learn and grow through my mistakes, God begins to give me His strength. Once I reach the place where He wants me to be, then God begins to bring me out of my wilderness.

Safe from Satan's Clutches

"How excellent is thy loving kindness, O God! Therefore the children of men put their trust under the shadow of thy wings." —Psalm 3:6-7

When I first read these verses, I could feel the warmth and comfort God was bringing to me. As I began to see God as my beautiful place of refuge, my thoughts began to drift off to a snowcapped mountain, and at the top of the mountain, I could see a cave that was surrounded by snow. The cave appeared to be a place of refuge from the storms.

In a similar way, I can see God standing before me, so beautiful and snowy white. I see His arms reaching out as He longs to be my place of refuge. Then I find myself walking into His arms of love and mercy as He instantly becomes the shelter from my storm.

As long as I remain in His arms of love, I know that His peace and security will continue to surround me and keep me close to His side, away from the clutches of Satan.

Faith in the Unseen God

"Whom having not seen, ye love; in whom though now ye see him not, yet believing, ye rejoice with joy unspeakable and full of glory." –I Peter 1:8

What faith we have, to be able to worship and love a God we cannot see! When we allow the unseen love to grow within us, we come to know Him more, as if we are viewing Him for the first time.

Words can never describe the feelings I experience when God becomes alive within me. I begin to think about the "Holy of Holies" mentioned in the Bible.

To me, this is a place where I can leave everything of myself out, so I can welcome God to work in and through me. My love for Him becomes my sacrifice to Him.

When I see Him begin to work and I see how God touches other hearts, then the joy I feel begins to lighten up my heart. It's as though a piece of Heaven came down and surrounded me.

Freed from Darkness

"For with thee is the fountain of life; in thy light shall we see light."
—Psalm 36:9

If it wasn't for God's powerful light, then we would always live in darkness. One day, while I was praying, I was thinking about the people I was praying for. I was thinking about the pain that some people experience, and then I was thinking about other people who live with loneliness. As I began to pray for each individual person, I was thinking about the darkness that comes along with each of these circumstances. Pain isn't from God and loneliness isn't from God either, so these circumstances have to be forms of darkness.

As I continued to pray, God showed me that His light is what makes darkness leave; so I began to pray that God's Holy light would shine down on each person who was hurting, so God could either heal them or His light would sustain them.

We, as children of the Most High God, do not have to stay in darkness. All we have to do is pray or talk to God or read

His word, and then our relationship with Him will become something close and special. When we choose to do this, then we will always be in the light, and no matter what we may be going through at the time, His light will always be there to keep the darkness away.

Letting Go, To Gain God

"But what things were gain to me, those I counted loss for Christ." —
Philippians 3:7

Through many painful moments of my life, God taught
me that I would have to let go of my own wants and desires
so I could make room for His desires instead.

There were many disappointments in my life and there
were many dreams I wanted to come true, but I knew that if I
wanted God to work in and through me, I would have to give
them up for Him.

I began to realize even more that if I took charge and
made my desires above God's, then I could not serve God.
God gave me a choice and, even though other women were
having children and lived mostly pain free, I knew that God's
desire for me was to be trained for His service. Even though
it was hard for me to give up so much in my life, God seemed
to be filling me with Himself even more.

Sometimes when we experience overwhelming loss in our
lives, this could be a symptom that God has something spe-

cial for us, so keep focused on God, instead of your circumstance, then you won't miss out on His blessings for your life.

Leaving My Pathway for His

"Those things, which ye have both learned, and received, and heard, and seen in me, do; and the God of peace shall be with you." –John 4:9

We, as Christians, seem to make life harder than what God intended life to be. God has given us His word as an example or tool to follow in our lives. All we have to do is obey Him as He speaks His words of truth into our hearts.

He showed us the example of His own life before He went to the cross, and then He died to take away our sins and show us His love. All we have to do is accept His truth and His truth will free us from the problems we face each day.

We wonder why we don't have peace when we are praying for His peace. If we aren't experiencing His peace, it could be because we are not walking close enough to Him. Maybe it's because we are following our own pathway instead of His. What God has taught me is that His benefits come from simply obeying Him and His word.

If we aren't experiencing His peace, then we need to get off our own pathway and seek out His. As we begin to follow after His lead, then we will truly experience that perfect peace because, after all, we are walking with the "Prince of Peace."

Always and Forever

"For all the flesh is as grass, and all the glory of man as the flower of grass. The grass withereth, and the flower there of falleth away; But the word of the Lord endureth forever. And this is the word which by the gospel is preached unto you."
—I Peter 1:24-25

Even though we may give up certain things in this world for God, we never lose touch with God. Even though evil tries to strip us of the things that are dear to our hearts, evil cannot remove God from us as long as we choose to remain close to God.

In my own life, I wasn't able to have children and I wasn't able to continue the things I enjoyed as a child, like ice skating, playing tennis, or just running down the road and riding my bike. As I went through multiple knee surgeries, I gave up the bending of my right knee in exchange for a rod, but God wasn't taken away with those things. In fact, God has become even stronger than before.

Circumstances in our lives can strip us of the things we once enjoyed to a point where we feel alone and helpless, but one thing we need to remember is that God is still there and He always will remain there.

Rising above Troubles

"Thou, which hast shewed me great and sore troubles, shalt quicken me again, and shalt bring me up again from the depths of the earth. Thou shalt increase my greatness and comfort me on every side." –Psalm 71: 20-21

God has shown me that, no matter what I go through in this life, His hand remains on the circumstance. There is no other power that is greater than the power of God.

God sometimes allows Satan to work, but God still has the control stick in His hand. I have felt God's presence, time after time, as He began to set up boundaries in my life so Satan could not cross and do further damage. When God had finished setting up the boundaries He took the circumstance that Satan had placed in my way and He used my weakness to make me stronger in Him.

Throughout the difficult moments in my life, God was teaching me to exchange my weaknesses for His greater strength instead of allowing the moments of despair to swallow me up.

God began to speak to my heart and He showed me that if I wanted to exchange my weakness for His strength, then I would have to pray and talk with Him more and seek Him in a stronger way. Then, as I begin to follow Him more, I will begin to see the rainbow of His love more clearly and the storms in my life will begin to cease.

A Heart of Thanksgiving

"Be careful for nothing; but in everything by prayer and supplication with thanksgiving let your requests be made known unto God." — Philippians 4:6

God showed me that when I pray I should pray with a heart of thanksgiving. This way I'm letting God know that I believe in His awesome power. In other words, I'm seeing my prayers go up to Him in a more powerful way as doubt begins to leave.

God taught me that I needed to bring my needs to Him and thank Him for what He was about to do. When I pray like this, I feel like I am leaving the need more with Him. He may not always answer my prayers in the way I would like, but, at the same time, I know that I am letting His will be done. We need to spiritually leave our needs in His lap of love, and then walk away with a confidence that He will do what's best.

Positive Thoughts

"Enter not into the path of the wicked, and go not in the way of evil men. Avoid it, pass not by it, turn from it, and pass away." –Proverbs 4:14-15

When God showed me these verses for the first time, a picture immediately appeared within my mind. I could see God up in Heaven above me and evil below me. When I talked to God or read His word or perceived something in a positive way, then I became closer to Him, where Satan couldn't bother me. But on the other hand, if I began to get caught up in the world in a bad way, then I began to lower myself into the clutches of Satan.

During our devotions, my husband and I were talking and we were saying to each other that sometimes we feel like Satan keeps pouncing and pouncing on us. As we began to talk more, God showed me that we should get rid of Satan right away when he attacks us. The more we leave our heart's door open to him, the more he will add to what he's already done. God showed me that if we want to remain out of the clutches of Satan, then we will have to fix our attention totally on God.

Finding God

"The Lord is nigh unto them that are of a broken heart; and saveth such as be of a contrite spirit. Many are the afflictions of the righteous; but the Lord delivereth him out of them all." —Psalm 34:18-19

The first time I found these verses, I began to realize that God was showing me that He was much closer during the more painful moments. The more I read these verses, the more I began to feel His comforting spirit as He continued to reassure me that He would always be there for me.

I found these verses around the time I was beginning my counseling for sexual abuse, and I believe that these two verses had become another lifeline for me. If I wouldn't have known that God was so close to me during one of the roughest times of my life, then I would have felt completely lost.

We know that God is always near, but isn't it comforting to know that He will bend down and be the Father that comforts His child when they are wounded and afraid?

Trusting God's Ways

"The Lord redeemeth the soul of his servants; and none of them that trust in him shall be desolate." Psalm 34:22

I've gone down some rugged pathways in my life and I feel that I wouldn't have had to endure some of those moments if I would have trusted God more.

One day, as I was talking to God and getting around for the day, I began to apologize to Him for all the wasted moments in my life. I don't know what happened that day, but I began to see all the wasted days that could have been spent doing the right thing instead of my own thing.

God showed me through time that if I would've simply trusted Him, instead of trying to figure Him out, then He would've helped me a lot sooner.

How many times do we try to figure out a God who made all things, including us? All God expects of us is to give Him our best; then He will take what we have given Him and He will meet us there and crown our efforts with His success, according to His plan.

Suffering for a Reason

"If ye be reproached for the name of Christ, happy are ye; for the spirit of glory and of God resteth upon you; on their part he is evil spoken of, but on your part he is glorified." –I Peter 4:14

What an honor to be chosen to suffer for the cause of Christ. When I was young, little did I know that God had plans for my life. At first, I thought that I was just going through an ordinary health problem with my knees.

Later in my life, God showed me something different. He began to slowly reveal to me that He had a plan laid out for me since the day He fashioned me in my Mother's womb. Little did I know that I would have to endure this much so I could find His desires for my life.

There were many difficult days that made me want to give up, but then God would remind me about His death on the cross. He reminded me how He was brutally beaten, with nails in His hands and feet; the Roman Soldiers pushed a crown of thorns into His skull and thrust a sword into His side. With all the pain and agony He went through, Jesus never gave up; instead He went through all of this pain just to say, "I Love You!"

It's so easy to say, "I Love You Jesus," but can we still say, "I Love You Jesus" when there's pain or hard times in our life? I began to see that if Jesus could give Himself up for me, then I could do the same for Him.

Rescued by God

"The steps of a good man are ordered by the Lord; and he delighteth in his way. Though he fall, he shall not be utterly cast down: for the Lord upholdeth him with his hand." —Psalm 37: 23-24

When I read the portion of these verses that says, "Though he fall, he shall not be utterly cast down; for the Lord upholdeth him with his hand," I thought of God in Heaven, for He's always watching over His children, and the moment He sees one of His children fall, His Almighty hands reach down to lift us back up so we can continue on His pathway.

Have you ever had a time in your life when you said to yourself, if it hadn't been for God, then I would've never made it? You made it because God heard your cry and reached out His hand of love and caught you, even in the midst of your despair. I can see several instances in my own life that I couldn't imagine where I'd be if it wasn't for the strong hands of God, reaching down to save me.

Where in this world can we find such love? It's so easy to get caught up in our circumstance that we forget that God is there for us whenever we need Him. Let God become stronger than your circumstance and then you will never lose sight of Him.

Finding New Life Through His Death

"For I through the law am dead to the law, that I might live unto God. I am crucified with Christ; nevertheless I live; yet not I, but Christ liveth in me; and the life which I now live in the flesh I live by the faith of the Son of God, who loved me, and gave himself for me. I do not frustrate the grace of God; for if righteousness come by the law, then Christ is dead in vain." –Galatians 2: 19-21

Through many hard moments of my life, God has shown me that I need to be as one with Him if I expect to make it through my life. When I give up the pleasures of my own life, so that I can be pleasing to God, then I have shown God that He is all I desire. As I let go of my own wants, then I have made room for God's desires to be seen through me, as He works out His plan for my life.

When we, as Christians, choose to follow the ways of the world, then everything Christ died for becomes in vain. Instead of Christ being seen in us, we become a person that's walking around with a sign on our foreheads that says "Christian." God just doesn't want us to advertise; He wants us to show the real thing to the world, which is Jesus.

The God of All Things

"I will bless the Lord, who hath given me counsel; my reins also instruct me in the night seasons. I have set the Lord always before me; because he is at my right hand, I shall not be moved." —Psalm 16:7-8

Throughout the years, I have found God to be so many things in my life, but, most of all, I've found Him to be my "Spiritual Physician" when I'm in pain because He sustains me when the doctors have done all they can do. I've found Him to be my "Prince of Peace" when I feel frustrated with life and then He becomes a "Great Counselor" when I need a friend to talk to.

One of the best things I love about God is that He is open to my call, twenty-four hours a day and seven days a week. He never closes for holidays and never takes a vacation and, even better, I never have to pay for the call because He already paid the price when He died on the cross.

When I am close to God, I know that He will never allow anything to hurt or destroy me, unless it's for my good. I have found God to be a close friend who is always waiting for me with outstretched arms. What a great feeling to know that in His presence, everything is alright and all I need is what He provides.

Exchanging Fear for His Perfect Love

"There is no fear in love; but perfect love casteth out fear; because fear hath torment. He that feareth is not made perfect in love." –I John 4:18

"Perfect love casteth out fear;" God showed me that if I wanted fear and doubt and other negative feelings to leave, then I would have to find the perfect love that only comes from God.

He showed me that negative feelings and positive feelings can't work together as one, and if I held tight to the negative things of this world, then I couldn't experience a close, loving relationship with Him.

He taught me that the only way I could get rid of fear in my life was to seek out His perfect love. As I began to seek, I found myself singing to God in the morning and evening hours. I began to find myself talking to Him, like I would a close friend, and then I began to dig deeper in His word for the hidden treasures that I had missed throughout the past years. God revealed to me that there was more truth hidden below the surface of my life and I needed to keep searching.

If a person wanted to dive for hidden treasure in the ocean, he wouldn't just put on his gear and float on the surface of the water. No, he would have to dive deep below the surface so he could find the hidden treasure. This is what God wants us to do in our own lives. If we dive deeper in His word then He will show us the hidden treasure of His truth that can set us free forever.

Suffering for Jesus

"For unto you it is given in the behalf of Christ, not only to believe on him, but also to suffer for his sake; Having the same conflict which ye saw in me, and now here to be in me." —Philippians 1:29-30

When I accepted Jesus into my life, I accepted Him because I believed in who He was and is. He was the Messiah that came into the world so in the end He could show His amazing love to us through His death on the cross.

When I began to suffer with my knee problems, I wondered if God had stopped loving me. After all, how could a God of love still allow so much to happen in my life?

As I began to search deeper into God's word, I began to understand how easy it is to become a Christian and say, "I Love You Jesus," but when one circumstance after another comes, is that love still the same? No one could ever suffer like Jesus suffered, as He gave up His whole life for us just so He could say, "I Love You." I began to see our suffering in a similar way. If we are going to say, "I Love You, Jesus," we should be able to say it and feel it in the same way when we are going through the roughest storms of our life.

Waiting for His Best

"Wait on the Lord, and keep his way, and he shall exalt thee to inherit the land; when the wicked are cut off, thou shalt see it." —*Psalm 37:34*

Through time I've learned to wait on God before making any decisions in my life. I truly believe that God will do His best for us when we choose to wait on Him.

I've learned that the pathway walked down with the Most High God can go from smooth to rocky. A smooth pathway appears when life is going well and we are blessed by God. A rocky pathway appears when trials arrive in our lives.

The rocky pathway can seem hard to cross; that's why we need to always stay a footstep behind God, because there may be a time when we will need His help and guidance. We also need to remain close to God when the pathway seems clear, otherwise we may miss out on the blessings that God has in store for us.

Either way, we need to let God do the leading while we follow; that way we are always able to find His footprints as He leads us through His will.

Leave it with God

"Take therefore no thought for the morrow; for the morrow shall take thought for the things of itself. Sufficient unto the day is the evil thereof."
—Matthew 7:34

Why do we, as people, leave the present moment only to worry about a moment that is either gone or hasn't arrived?

There were many times that I would sit down on a Sunday evening and think about everything I had to do for the rest of the week. I was mentally drained and filled with worry before I even began the week.

God showed me through this verse that I had enough to think of for the day I was living. Many times we worry about the future and when we finally reach that moment, God ends up taking us in a whole different direction and all the previous moments we worried were for nothing.

God brought to my attention that when we worry about our yesterdays, then it's as if God is looking down and saying, "What are you talking about?" In a similar way, when we worry about the days ahead of us, it's as if God is looking down and saying, "I haven't even created that day for you to live, so why worry needlessly my child?"

If we are so busy worrying about the past and future, then we may also miss the blessings that God has for us today...blessings that could lift us out of our overwhelming circumstances.

Waiting for His Help

"Wait on the Lord; be of good courage, and he shall strengthen thine heart; wait, I say, on the Lord." –Psalm 27:14

Waiting on God can be so difficult, but I learned that if we aren't following right behind Jesus then we begin to lose sight of Him. His footprints become less noticeable and we find ourselves hopelessly lost.

When we grow impatient and we don't wait for Jesus, then we begin to move way ahead of Him, and then when we need His help we find ourselves like lost sheep that can't find their way back.

When we choose to follow right behind Jesus, and we begin to need His strength and courage, we will be close enough so He will be able to give us what we need as we journey with Him, and His provisions will become a way of sustaining us until He can remove the "thorn of suffering."

I found that all I need to do is wait for Jesus and let Him become my life. Once I have His life within me, then He will become my truth so I can be free from the deceiving lies of

Satan; then He will become my way and His way will lead me to Heaven.

The Tears of a Broken Heart

"Depart from me, all ye workers of iniquity; for the Lord hath heard the voice of my weeping. The Lord hath heard my supplication; the Lord will receive my prayers." –Psalm 6:8-9

God not only sees the tears that fall from our eyes, but I believe that He also sees the tears that flow from our hearts within. I believe that God can look deep within us and know the thoughts that produce our tears.

We can just sit or kneel in prayer and He will hear us, but I have come to also realize that through my own moments of pain, He touches us in a way we sometimes don't see or imagine. I have found myself sitting alone on my bed and then, as I began to cry out to God, it seemed that I could begin to sense the arms of God around me as He would whisper in my ear, "It's going to be alright, my child."

How many times do we truly seek deep for God during the painful moments in our life? We could avoid needless despair by just whispering His name, "Jesus."

God's Deliverance

"He delivered me from my strong enemy, and from them which hated me; for they were too strong for me." –Psalm 18:17

God brought this verse to me as a reminder that when a circumstance becomes too large for me to handle, He is the one who can be stronger for me.

No matter what may be coming against me or no matter what I'm going through, God is stronger and nothing can supersede His power.

I have seen God lift me out of the clutches of Satan's hands many times. When I was in a pit of despair, it was God who walked by that pit and rescued me.

How many times do we either sit in the pit of despair and give up or try to climb out on our own? When we try to make our life work on our own, it's as if we are trying to climb up the rugged walls of our pit. When we try to do it alone, we continually find ourselves falling back because we don't have enough of our own strength.

When we find ourselves at the bottom of the pit, then it's time to call out to God. He will walk over to our pit of despair and He will reach His hand down into the pit and say, "I know you are weak, my child; let me be the strength you need."

Returning our Love

"Because he hath set his love upon me, therefore will I deliver him; I will set him on high, because he hath known my name. He shall call upon me, and I will answer him: I will be with him in trouble; I will deliver him, and honor him." —Psalms 91: 14-15

I know that when I have a close relationship with God, He will always be close to me and be there to help in times of need.

If I wanted to make a new friend and my new friend wanted to share in the friendship, then I wouldn't take advantage of my new friend and walk away; no, I would love that new friend and share together in the relationship.

Life with God is similar; we shouldn't just ask for His help and never love Him. He wants to bless us and help us, but first of all God wants our friendship and love. He wants to be able to feel our love for Him, as we feel His love touching our hearts.

The only one who really knows the real depth of God's name is the one who talks with Him daily; he is the one who is always searching for God's truth, and he is the one who hasn't seen God but can know Him by the way God touches him each day.

Communing Heart to Heart

"He that dwelleth in the secret place of the Most High shall abide under the shadow of the Almighty." –Psalm 91:1

When I think of my secret place with God, I picture a place in my mind that is similar to the "Holy of Holies." This place becomes my refuge, where only God and I meet. My secret place with God is where I am able to leave the world out and commune with God alone. This is a place where I can be myself before God and He will never walk away. This beautiful place is where God may tell me some of the plans He has for my life. This place is where I can cry out to God and I know that He will hear me because He is so near to me.

We all should have a place in our minds where we can meet with God on a more personal level, where we can tell God our needs and other problems that we may not share with others. What a place to find peace with God, where we can feel safe and free from all evil. As we fellowship with God, under the shadow of the Almighty, we begin to feel a piece of Heaven enter our spirits.

Chastened for a Reason

"The Lord hath chastened me sore; but he hath not given me over unto death." –Psalm 118:18

When I look back at all the painful moments in my life, I realize now that God was chastening and remolding me according to the plan He had purposed for me.

There were times that I would cry out to God and say to Him, "I feel like I'm going to die," or "Oh God, I'm not making it," but then God would speak to my heart and say, "Diane, you're making it because you are still living out your life." It was at that moment that I truly understood this verse, "The Lord hath chastened me sore; but he hath not given me over unto death."

From that moment on, I knew that I could make it. All I had to do was let God do His work, in and through me. Even though the moments weren't always easy, I knew for the first time what God was doing in my life and the moments I went through reassured me that everything was going to be alright.

When I go through a trial now, I know that God is at work exchanging my weakness for His strength.

Growing through Pain

"Before I was afflicted I went astray; but now have I kept thy word. It is good for me that I have been afflicted; that I might learn thy statutes." –Psalm 119:67, 71

How do we learn God's ways, unless we experience them first? I've had people ask me, "If you wouldn't have gone through all of the painful moments in your life, would you be as close to God, as you are now?" I always responded, "No!" I didn't just make it where I am today with God. His strength and goodness came through hard times and lessons learned.

I picture my life as a staircase to Heaven. Some of the steps are easier to climb and some of them are more difficult. Through painful moments, I began to realize that I was either going to sit in my "ashes of despair" and stay on the steps or I was going to depend on God to help me up the next step. That's when God made it my choice.

As I started to climb up the steps, I realized that each step became easier when I thought about the lessons that were learned on previous steps. As I continue to climb the steps and learn, I know that eventually the steps will lead me home to Heaven.

Allowing God to Take Over

"For by thee I have run through a troop; and by my God have I leaped over a wall." –Psalm 18:29

Throughout the past years of my life, God has taught me that I can do anything with His help. I've learned that I am just a shell of a person and I'm not able to do anything unless I allow God to come in and fill me with Himself. I can't think without His wisdom and I can't see without looking through His eyes and only His words fill my ears and thoughts. My hands and legs move only by His command.

God showed me that when I don't allow Him to work in me, then it's as if I have tied up His hands and feet and made Him blind and deaf.

When I think of this verse, I picture myself as a runner. My own strength is too weak to jump over the obstacles of my life, but when I let my own ways die, then I have made more room for God to enter, and once He has entered, then I can spiritually leap over any obstacle that gets in my way.

You may be physically or spiritually weak to the point that you can't find the strength you need to leap over life's obstacles, but remember God has enough strength for everyone, with more to spare.

Reaching Out through Affliction

"Unless thy law had been my delights, I should then have perished in mine affliction. I will never forget thy precepts; for with them thou hast quickened me." –Psalm 119:92-93

Many times I've thought, "Where would I be today, if it wasn't for Jesus?" Through each difficult trial in my life, God has given me something new to exchange for my failures.

Let's say that you wanted to plant a tree and you wanted the tree to become strong and beautiful. The tree would need to be pruned back, so when spring comes, the new shoots would bring new growth to the tree. If you were to continually prune the tree, then over a period of time, the tree would become stronger and more beautiful.

This illustration is similar to our own lives. There may be moments that God needs to spiritually prune us back through different circumstances, but we learn from the difficult moments and we come out of our circumstances stronger than before. The more God prunes us, then the stronger we will become for Him.

A Special Love

"My son, despise not the chastening of the Lord; neither be weary of his correction: For whom the Lord loveth he correcteth; even as a Father the son in whom he delighteth." —Proverbs 3:11-12

God used the words in these verses to bring a special peace to my mind. When I first went through the beginning of my surgeries, I didn't seem to understand what God was doing. All I knew was that I was going through dislocations, surgeries, and very painful moments in my life. I didn't know what God had planned for me, until I was in my late thirties.

As the surgeries became more frequent, I began to wonder if God loved me anymore. After all, why didn't this God of great power just heal my legs?

As I began to search the Bible for the answer to my question, God showed me these two verses. I learned that God was using the painful moments in my life to remold me into a vessel that could be used later for His honor and glory. The harder the circumstance became, the more God was reshaping me for Him. A bond began to form between God and I that made my love for Him become even stronger than before. He became my spiritual Father and I became His spiritual daughter.

He wasn't correcting me as a means of hurting me. He was correcting me so I could learn to walk down His pathways, instead of my own. He was using the weaknesses in my life to produce a stronger growth. I began to see my circumstances in a different way. Instead of feeling that He was against me, I began to feel His love become stronger instead.

Strength through Adversity

"If thou faint in the day of adversity, thy strength is small." —
Proverbs 24:10

There were times when I would get so easily upset, especially when I found out that I was facing another knee surgery. The surgeries became an old thing after awhile. What seemed small to another person became big and blown out of proportion in my eyes.

One day I found Proverbs 24:10 and the words in this verse began to stand out and become a stronger verse to me. I began to see that each moment I got upset was because my strength wasn't strong enough. I found that there was more of Diane in me than God. Through time, God taught me to slow down and lean on His strength instead of my own.

I'll never be perfect in this life. We all live with our own little flaws, but if we can take the wisdom God gives us, we can use His wisdom as a tool to fix the moments of failure in our life.

I Was Blinded but Now I See

"I have heard of thee by the hearing of the ear; but now mine eye seeth thee." —Job 42:5

The book of Job has been such an inspiration to me. Job had riches and everything he needed in life, but when God allowed all of his possessions to leave him, Job was put through a great time of testing until Job came to realize that God was more powerful than all he once possessed. Once Job learned this, God blessed Job with even more than before.

It's so easy to have Jesus close beside us when everything is at its worst, but what do we do with Him at other times? God showed me that to know Him is more than just knowing of Him. He didn't just want me when it was convenient for me. He wanted me to see Him for the God He truly is.

I began to see God's truth and I learned to talk to Him more often, and not just in prayer. I began to share my life with Him in a personal way, and in time, my love for Him became richer. Now I talk to Jesus just like I would with anyone else. The moment I began to treat Him like my best friend, in return, He began to share His great wisdom with me.

Jesus paid a terrible price for us just because He loved us. No matter what we may be going through for the moment, now it's our turn to show our love for Him.

Lifted Up With Love

"Fear thou not; for I am with thee; be not dismayed; for I am thy God: I will strengthen thee; yea, I will help thee; yea, I will uphold thee with the right hand of my righteousness." – Isaiah 41:10

When we have God in our life, we are never alone because He is watching over us all the time. He helped me to understand, that even though He couldn't free me from my circumstance, still it was God who was holding my hand and sustaining me through the worst moments.

As I look back on all I've been through, I'm sure it wasn't easy for God to just stand by and see all that was taking place in my life, but He had a plan to strengthen me and, until that plan was accomplished, He remained close by.

Before I entered the operating room to have the rod put into my right leg, I remember asking God to be close to me, near the operating table. Even though the operating room was full of all kinds of scary instruments, I still felt His peace, and I knew He was right there beside me.

The Mighty Warrior

"And they shall fight against thee; but they shall not prevail against thee; for I am with thee, saith the Lord, to deliver thee." —Jeremiah 1:19

Through many difficult moments, God showed me that He was still in charge. Even though I felt His distance at times, He had His ways of showing me that He was still there.

I believe that God allows what Satan does to better us and make us stronger people. The more I see God at work in my life, the more I long to turn to Him. Moments like these have helped me to see God for who He really is, even though I can't see Him with my eyes. He has become my mighty warrior, and He's the one that comes down from Heaven to free me from the evil that surrounds me.

When I've seen God lift me out of my moments of despair, my love for Him becomes something special. His love has become a love that I thought I'd never experience in my lifetime. The love I feel is like a piece of Heaven that has come down to me and has become my rock, where God and I become as one.

God Wins Over Temptation

"Jesus said unto him, it is written again, Thou shalt not tempt the Lord thy God." –Matthew 4:7

This verse comes from the story of Jesus, when He was tempted by Satan in the wilderness. When Satan tried to tempt Jesus, Jesus came right to the point with Satan so Satan would have to leave. Jesus didn't get caught up in a long, drawn out discussion with Satan and He didn't allow the temptation to continue in His thoughts either. When Jesus walked away from Satan, He had a settled feeling because He knew that the words He spoke to Satan were full of power and truth.

After reading this verse, I discovered that I was going through needless moments of confusion and frustration because I was allowing Satan's words to affect my thoughts. The more I dwelt on the issues, the more I began to open up my hearts door to Satan. I had to learn to open the door to Jesus and allow His peace and goodness to reign in my heart, otherwise Satan would work his way in and bring all his filth with him. I've learned that if I don't ignore Satan, then God will not have enough room to work in my life.

Finding the Need Instead of the Fault

"But I say unto you, Love your enemies, bless them that curse you, do good to them that hate you, and pray for them which despitefully use you, and persecute you;" Matthew 5:44 "For if you love them which love you, what reward have ye? Do not even the publicans the same?" —Matthew 5:46

Loving our enemies can be the hardest thing to do. God taught me that if I only love those who love me, then what reward can I receive from loving that way?

The real love of God comes from a heart of God, who sees the need more than the fault. How is it that people only make friends with those who are smart, good looking, or with those who dress the best? Jesus taught me that loving man means to reach out to all people, just like He did and would, even to this day. If we are only reaching out to those who love us, then who is going to share God's love with the other people?

I had a neighbor once and he was a hard-core man. He would barely say "hi" to my husband and me. One day, I was talking with God and I said, "Please Lord, help me to love that man." To make a long story short, one day I was outside working on something and I heard a voice say, "Hi, Diane." I couldn't believe it, that man was saying "hi" to me. Now he's a Christian and he's reaching out to help others. What a surprise! See, it does pay to love your enemies and pray for them too.

Losing Ourselves to Gain God

"He that findeth his life shall lose it; and he that loseth his life for my sake shall find it." –Matthew 10:39

God used this verse in a very profound way so I could find Him deeper in my life. While other people were enjoying their lives, I was either in the hospital or I was laid up at home. While other women were having children, I was childless.

During the more difficult moments, I would say to God, "Is there anything else you want to take from me?" At that time, I had no idea what God was doing, until He began to finally show me that He had a different plan for my life. He taught me that I would have to be willing to give up all my wants so I could have His desires for my life.

I look back on my life now and I'm glad that God followed through with His plan! I can truthfully say that I am glad to be where I am in life because I have found a real good friend, who is Jesus. The empty voids that have been empty for so long are now filled with God's presence. I found that it's better to lose some of life's pleasures now and have God in the end, than to have everything now and lose God later.

Used for a Purpose

"And as Jesus passed by, he saw a man which was blind from his birth, and his disciples asked him, saying, Master who did sin, this man, or his parents, that he was born blind? Jesus answered, 'Neither hath this man sinned, nor his parents; but that the works of God should be made manifest in him.'" —John 9:1-3

People suffer for different reasons. I believe that God allows illness and heartache as a means of drawing someone closer to Him, but most of all, I believe that God uses our circumstances in a weaker way so His strength can be seen in a more profound way.

My knee problems were a congenital problem from birth. I feel that God formed me this way in my Mother's womb because He had a plan from the start, to use this weak circumstance so He could make Himself seen for a greater purpose.

Through difficult moments, God showed me that I would have to give up myself so I could have His heart to understand the needs and feelings of others who hurt. If I used my own heart to help people, they would never see Jesus.

God never wastes what He allows. There's a purpose for everything under Heaven. If you are going through a lot in your life, then go to the one who holds the answers to our questions. That one is Jesus. He holds the keys that can unlock our hearts and set us free.

Walking in His Footprints

"I am the vine, ye are the branches; He that abideth in me, and I in him, the same bringeth forth much fruit; for without me ye can do nothing." —John 15:5

What a great illustration God gives us in this verse. If a person had a desire to grow grapes, he would plant them, water them, and do whatever it takes to produce the best grapes. If the branches and the vines didn't appear, there would be no grapes to harvest.

God has taught me something similar to this: if I choose to go my own way without God, there won't be any help and guidance. If there's no help and guidance, I wouldn't begin to understand another hurting heart.

God has made a pathway for me so I can follow in His footprints, and He is the one who walks ahead of me. When the road is hard, He makes the load lighter by carrying me on His shoulders as He sustains me. When I don't know what detour to take, He leads me in the right direction, and when I need a little encouragement, He lays His hand on my shoulder as He speaks words of peace into my ear. When this long and narrow pathway comes to an end, I will have reached my destination with Him in Heaven.

Chosen through Love

"Ye have not chosen me, but I have chosen you, and ordained you, that ye should go and bring forth fruit, and that your fruit should remain; that whatsoever ye shall ask of the Father in my name, he may give it you." –John 15:16

Can you imagine a God of such love and perfection choosing us, with all our little imperfections? What an honor and privilege it is to serve such a God of great love!

When we accept Jesus into our hearts, our minds are telling us that we chose Him but, really, it was Jesus who chose us. Jesus has such a deep love for us that He overlooks our little imperfections. All He wants to do is love and accept us for who we are.

God taught me that I can't serve Him and be blessed in my life and ministry if I can't follow His example first. How can I reach out to others and bring them to God if I am judging them more than loving them? We need to stop and think before we judge others and we need to ask ourselves, would this be something that Jesus would do?

Letting Go for God

"If ye were of the world, the world would love his own; but because ye are not of the world, but I have chosen you out of the world, therefore the world hateth you." –John 15:19

There are two different ways we live in this life. One way is for the world and the other way is for God. When we first become a Christian, we begin to think with a heart that desires to do great things for God. The old ways of the past begin to dim out and we begin to look through the eyes of God.

Just as Jesus was hated and rejected, we too, begin to feel hated and rejected for following the ways of Jesus. When we can rise above the difficult moments and stay grounded in Jesus, we become victorious through Him, and our love for Him begins to be on a more solid foundation where Satan's clutches can't reach.

Even through persecution, Jesus showed us just how much He was willing to give up on the cross so His love could be seen by us. When we show trust and courage during the hardest storms of our life, we are showing God that we have truly laid down our own life for His.

There to the End

"And being fully persuaded that, what he had promised, he was able also to perform." –Romans 4:21

God is a God of His word. When He is using a circumstance in our life to make us stronger for Him, He may take His time but, in the end, He will complete what He started.

An illustration could be a puzzle. When a puzzle is being assembled and only a portion of the puzzle is done, then there would be no way to view the whole picture. The puzzle may take time, but when the whole puzzle is finished, the full picture of the puzzle will show its hidden beauty.

This example is similar to us and how God works in our lives. Sometimes God takes His time so all of our pieces can be put right where He designed them to be. When God puts in the final piece, He has completed His handiwork; His beauty can be seen through us. If He was to leave something undone, the full picture of His plan for us would not be seen.

One So True

"What shall we then say to these things? If God be for us, who can be against us? He that spared not his own Son, but delivered him up for us all, how shall he not with him also freely give us all things?" – Romans 8:31-32

God freely gave His only Son so He could pay the price for every sin in our life. He did this so His great love could be seen. Can you imagine how He must have felt when He saw His only Son suffer in such a brutal way? I wonder if God was crying when He saw His only Son hanging on a cross.

In so many words God is saying to me, "If I am willing to allow my only Son to die that you may see the great love I have for you, then why am I not able to help you in your life? Am I only a limited God?"

I began to see how hard it must have been for God. If such a great God was willing to sacrifice His only Son just to free me and love me, He could do anything and everything He desired for me.

Now as I look through His eyes, I see a brand new meaning; when the trees blow in the wind and the stars dance in the sky and as rain produces tear drops from Heaven, what I'm feeling is the presence of One so true.

His Love Conquers All

"As it is written, for thy sake we are killed all the daylong; we are accounted as sheep for the slaughter. Nay, in all these things we are more than conquerors through him that loved us." –Romans 8:36-37

As I went through surgery after surgery, I felt so drained and I began to feel that all the strength I once had was gone. I wondered if my body could come back after all I had been through.

God showed me that through His strength I could get through anything, but if I wasn't willing to rise above myself, how would I find His strength to conquer all that was ahead of me?

I began to take my eyes off all the overwhelming circumstances that surrounded me and began to place my focus on God. Instead of thinking about the negative thoughts that were related to my circumstance, I started to seek what God had for me for that moment. Once I started to do this, the weight of my circumstance became lighter and my love for

God became stronger. By letting go, I was also able to give God a chance to work.

Since Jesus has become a closer friend, I no longer live in the dark, deep pit of circumstance. All I feel now is the light of His presence.

Made Weak to Help the Weak

"To the weak became I as weak, that I might gain the weak; I am made all things to all men that I might by all means save some." —I Corinthians 9:22

It's amazing how God uses different circumstances in our lives so that we can reach out and help others. Sometimes when God begins to work with us, He allows us to go down to a weaker state, and as we become spiritually stronger, He uses our painful experiences so the pain we once felt can be used to understand and touch another hurting heart.

I would never have the heart God gave me to share and help others if it wasn't for Him showing me the way first, through painful moments in my own life.

When the painful moments of my past begin to help another person who is hurting, the person I help can relate and share with others who hurt, too. From there, the person who learned from me can share the wisdom they learned with another person who is hurting. After a while, the chain of events becomes like a wild fire.

We may not want to go through the painful moments in our lives but in order for us to understand the need of another, we must continue on, until God is finished with us.

Comforting the Broken Hearted

"Who comforteth us in all our tribulation, that we may be able to comfort them which are in any trouble, by the comfort where with we ourselves are comforted of God." —II Corinthians 1:4

When I was going through sexual abuse counseling, there were times that I could sense a presence that was so comforting. As I sat on my bed one day, I was hugging the bedpost, and I began to cry out to God for help. I remember the day so clear because it was as if God Himself had sat down on the bed next to me. I began to feel His comforting arms around me as He appeared to be saying, "My child, it will be alright."

Since then, I've asked God many times to give me a loving spirit that breaks in little tiny pieces so I may be able to comfort others in the way God has comforted me.

Can you imagine what this world would be like if everyone had that same broken heart for others? Instead of judging and hurting others, this world would be like one large set of arms stretching out to comfort one another.

Only One God

"Then he answered and spake unto me, saying, This is the word of the Lord unto Zerubbabel, saying, Not by might, nor by power, but by my spirit, saith the Lord of hosts." – Zechariah 4: 6

I seemed to always think I knew what God wanted for my life until one day God showed me something different. It was as if God was saying, "Diane, why do you always think you know what I'm going to do in your life?" After hearing His words, I began to think, "How do I know what God is doing when He is higher and greater than me?" After all, He is God! He was the one who made me and fashioned me His way so why was I trying to figure Him out? From that moment, I began to ask God what He wanted me to do and then I waited for His answers.

When we are walking with God and we try to run ahead of Him, we have left Him behind us and we quickly find ourselves alone in our circumstance.

Over time, I found the right pathway that God wanted me on and I began to gain His strength and wisdom because I allowed God to lead me down the right pathway.

Pressing On

"And let us not be weary in well doing, for in due season we shall reap, if we faint not." –Galatians 6:9

God has us on a pathway and sometimes the pathway can be rugged from our circumstances and sometimes the pathway can seem so smooth and beautiful.

When we are having good days, the sky turns a beautiful shade of blue and the flowers along the pathway are in all the colors of the rainbow and the pathway ahead appears to be smooth.

When God allows trials to come into our lives, the skies turn a dark shade of purple and all that can be seen along the pathway are prickly weeds. The pathway begins to show some rough spots and, when the trial becomes the roughest, there are piles of large rocks across the pathway. Even though we become drained and exhausted from climbing over the rocks, a ray of God's light begins to shine down upon us and God begins to fill our thoughts with a picture of a beautiful city called Heaven.

As He fills our minds with hope He says, "My children, I know the pathway has been hard and difficult. If you can make it a little further, I will bring you home, and you will live in my beautiful city of Heaven with me forever."

The journey God has you on may be hard, with no end in sight, but hold on my child; if you believe in God and you remain close to Him, you will be home soon. Cling to the hope He's given you and God will sustain you and help you through your journey.

Whatever God Starts He Finishes

"Being confident of this very thing, that he which hath begun a good work in you will perform it until the day of Jesus Christ." –Philippians 1:6

One of the greatest thoughts that God has given me during the darkest moments of my life is that He always finishes what He starts. God never leaves anything unfinished.

When I found myself caught up in the difficult moments of my circumstance, I couldn't see any end to my pain. I felt like I was going down a long, dark tunnel, and all that was ahead of me was more darkness and more pain.

One day, God gave me a glimpse of His light. He was saying to me, "Diane, do you believe in me?" I said, "Yes." Then He said, "Diane, if I'm the One that has made all things complete in my creation, wouldn't I also complete what I started in you?" All of a sudden, I felt something click within my thoughts! His truth had finally set my mind free. His light became brighter than the deception of darkness that Satan had placed within me, and His light has remained ever since that moment.

God can do the same for you! Just believe in Him, and remember, when God starts something in your life, He will always finish what He's begun.

Hurt for a Reason

"For it is God which worketh in you both to will and to do of his good pleasure." —Philippians 2:13

We need to remember that God is good, and when He allows circumstances to come into our lives it's because He has a reason and a plan. God has His plan for our lives in clear view and God isn't going to allow the pain in our lives to continue beyond His plan.

We aren't always able to see the circumstances, the same way He does because we can only see what is happening for the moment, but God knows everything because He is the One who holds the plan for our lives within His hands.

When we get caught up in the circumstance, we don't always look at our problems through the eyes of God. If we could let Him lead us through His Master Plan, He would be there to comfort and sustain us all the way. When we look at our circumstances with our own worldly eyes, then the circumstance becomes overwhelming and we gradually pull ourselves away from God.

Why can't we trust God? If we will take the time to slow down and lay ourselves in His lap of love, then He will be able to use our circumstance for the purpose He planned. When God created the different seasons of the year, He knew that each season could only last so long so the other seasons could be seen, too. Well, God knows just how long to use our pain before He begins something new in us.

Running for the Prize

"I press toward the mark for the prize of the high calling of God in Christ Jesus." –Philippians 3:14

Whenever I read this verse, I see a lot of runners lining up to compete for the grand prize. They start out pursuing a dream by working hard so they can run fast and be able to leap over all the hurdles in the competition.

Life can be that way, too. We find ourselves continually running through the race of life until God allows the hurdles of circumstance to be placed in front of us. At first we fall, but when we call out to Him for help, He hears our cries of desperation, and He fills us with His perfect strength so, together, we can rise above the hurdles of circumstance. When the race ends, our prize will be God and an eternal home in Heaven.

If we continually trust God, He will give us the strength to conquer any circumstance. We will be able to keep up the pace He desires for us until we reach our eternal prize in Heaven.

There may be times that Satan tries to trip us so we will fall, but we need to get up and keep going. If we stay in our "ashes of despair" too long, the clutches of Satan will continually keep us from our eternal prize. Instead, we need to lean on God in case we become spiritually injured; He will be there to carry us the rest of the way.

Leaving the Past Behind

"Brethren, I count not myself to have apprehended; but this one thing I do, forgetting those things which are behind, and reaching forth unto those things which are before," – Philippians 3:13

I know that I will never be perfect in this lifetime, but one thing I know is if I am going to be on the same pathway with God, I must leave my past behind me.

There were times that God took me into my past but that was only because He was the One leading me there. There are times that God will take us into the past so we can find a healing and be able to move forward with God.

It's a dangerous thing to get caught up in the past. When we live in the past, we are away from God and then we end up lost in despair. We lose sight of God, and we are no longer able to experience the blessings God has for us for that moment. If God isn't leading us into the past, Satan will enter and create more damage.

One thing I can say for sure: if you are lost in despair and you can't find your way back to God, just call out His name.

He will find you and lead you back to where He wants you to
be.

No Other but God

"If ye then be risen with Christ, seek those things which are above, where Christ sitteth on the right hand of God. Set your affection on things above, not on things on the earth. For ye are dead, and your life is hid with Christ in God." – Colossians 3: 1-3

Have you ever wondered why our days don't always seem to go right? It could be because we have become more caught up in the world's way of thinking, instead of God's.

When I'm focused on God and my thoughts are only desiring His will for my life, I will be lifted above my circumstances, and I will be placed on the rock that brings me closer to God.

If my thoughts and words are always on the negative things around me, I am going to be brought lower where I have a greater chance of falling into the clutches of Satan.

We aren't perfect people but God has shown me through some tough times that I need to aim my thoughts and words toward Heaven. I need to look through His eyes, hear with His ears, and think the thoughts that will cause me to rise above my circumstances so I will be free from Satan's clutches.

Leaving the World Behind

"Choosing rather to suffer affliction with the people of God, than to enjoy the pleasures of sin for a season." Hebrews 11:25

As I look back on my life, I'm glad that I went through all the painful moments in my life because all the painful moments I went through brought me closer to God.

Sometimes God has to take us and set us aside so He can work with us, one to one. Once He gets our attention, He begins to work as He strips away all the hard layers that were built up throughout our lives. When God removes each painful layer, He places Himself within each empty layer so we can be made stronger through Him.

When a potter is making a vase, he takes the clay that has no shape and He begins to work at molding the clay into a vase. The vase may take time and a lot of work but, through time, that old lump of clay will take the form of a beautiful vase. This is how God works so lovingly with us. His work may take time and we may grow impatient, but in the end we will all be made into beautiful vessels for Him.

Loving Hands

"And ye have forgotten the exhortation which speaketh unto you as unto children, My Son, despise not thou the chastening of the Lord, nor faint when thou art rebuked of him; For whom the Lord loveth he chasteneth, and scourgeth every son whom he receiveth." —Hebrews 12:5-6

It's not always easy to go through trials, but God is reminding us that whom the Lord loveth He will chasten or correct.

When we were children, our parents, out of love, would spank us if we did something wrong. This was their way of getting our attention to show us what we had done wrong so we would obey and do what's right the next time.

This short story is similar to God's ways. God loves us, and in order for Him to get our attention and teach us the things we need to know, sometimes He has to allow a painful circumstance into our life so we will do what He desires for us. This is God's way of taking us off the wrong detour so He can place us onto the right pathway...the pathway He chose for us from the very beginning.

We are drawn closer to God when we learn from Him and obey Him. From there, a relationship and a bond are formed as we become His children and He becomes our Father.

I Became Nothing to Gain Everything

"Humble yourselves therefore under the mighty hand of God, that he may exalt you in due time: Casting all your care upon him; for he careth for you." –I Peter 5:6-7

Pride does not work with God. He is God and nothing can rise above His awesome power. I've had to learn the lesson on pride many times in my life. Why do we, as humans, feel that we can handle our circumstances when we are really nothing in comparison to God?

I had to learn, that if I wanted God to work in my life I would have to become lower than Him so He could help me. When we show humbleness to God, we have sent Him a signal that lets Him know that we are willing to listen to Him instead of ourselves.

I see a pathway. God and I are the only ones on the pathway. He is leading and I am following, but as pride enters into my life, I move way ahead of God. I attempt to work on my own circumstance, and as I do, I start falling over my circumstance because my circumstance becomes too difficult for me to handle alone. I panic, and as I call out to God, I discover that He's way behind me, allowing me to see what I can do on my own. As He catches up to me, He talks to me in a loving way and says, "All you have to do is follow, my child. Let me lead you for I already know the way, and I will lead you on the right pathway. I will be there to provide for you and to protect you along the journey."

When we choose to let God lead us on the pathway, just at the right time, God will bless us with better pathways and He will cause us to rise up and become stronger people.

True Love

"My little children, let us not love in word, neither in tongue; but in deed and truth." –I John 3:18

Through many trying days of pain, I have found God to be my best friend! Our relationship did not come overnight. Instead, our relationship came through many painful moments in my life. I learned to depend on God instead of myself, and through that dependence on Him, I began to find Him as a personal friend.

I found that it's so easy to say, "I love you," to God, but if there is no action with the words, each word remains empty, with no meaning. When I tell my husband that I love him, how would he be able to feel the love I have for him without showing some form of action with my words? I place my love for him above myself, and I try to make his life better by cooking him a special meal, even if I don't always care for what I fix. When he sees what I've done, he knows my words are true.

What about God? When we tell Him that we love Him, do we live for ourselves or do we show that love to Him by placing God above ourselves? When Jesus was preparing to die on the cross, He didn't say, "I love you," and walk away. No, He said, "I love you," while He was being beaten. He said, "I love you," when the spikes were going through His hands and feet and when He had a crown of thorns pushed into His skull. Most of all, He said, "I love you," when He died a horrible death to pay the price for our sins.

Open the Door; God's Knocking

"Behold, I stand at the door, and knock; if any man hear my voice, and open the door, I will come in to him, and will sup with him, and he with me." –Revelation 3:20

One day, I was in quite a bit of pain and I began to feel depressed. I was so tired from all I had been going through.

As I was crying out to God, He began to show me a picture. In this picture, I began to look deep within my heart. As I continued to view what God was showing me, I began to hear a tapping noise. I couldn't figure out where that noise was coming from. At that moment, God began to show me that the noise I was hearing was someone knocking on my heart's door. I could see myself answering the door, and as I looked out the door, such a bright light came through, it was as if I knew it was Jesus. As I turned in His direction, He said, "Diane, I've been here, knocking at your heart's door. I could see your pain, so I came to help you." Darkness began to leave, and the light of His presence brought such peace that I knew at that very moment it was God that had repaired my broken heart.

Hearing God's Soft Voice

"Wherefore my beloved brethren, let every man be swift to hear, slow to speak, slow to wrath; for the wrath of man worketh not the righteousness of God." –James 1:19-20

How many times do we actually sit in a quiet spot and listen for God's voice as He speaks to our hearts? If we are always distracted by ourselves and others, how are we going to be able to hear the still, small voice of God?

God has a plan for everyone's life, but how are we suppose to understand His plan if we are always telling God what we think should happen in our lives?

God's words come to us on angels' wings and His words are softly spoken and full of truth and peace, but how are we to hear that soft-spoken voice if we are too busy to listen?

I've learned that I have to allow God to clean out all the clutter while I'm meditating on Him; then I must seek out His ways. When my own thoughts have vanished and I leave myself open to Him, then He is able to place His thoughts upon my heart.

Deliverance Through the Raging Storms

"Thou art my hiding place; thou shalt preserve me from trouble; thou shalt compass me about with songs of deliverance." —Psalm 32:7

As the raging storms began to take over, I found my God walking on the stormy seas to me. He saw that I was tired from the storms in my life, but yet He knew that the storms would produce a stronger person.

As the storms raged from all sides, God held my hand until the time of testing was over; He came over to me and said, "Peace be still," and the storms in my life began to cease.

The storms in your life may be raging, too, and you may feel that you can't make it another moment. Just remember to hold tight to the strong anchor that is Jesus. He will not allow the storms in your life to overtake you. He's just allowing the storms into your life so you may learn to depend more on Him. He wants you to gain His strength so you will become stronger for the days ahead and, most of all, He knows that the storms will bring you closer to Him.

Learning to Receive His Promise

"For ye have need of patience, that, after ye have done the will of God, ye might receive the promise." –Hebrews 10:30

Whatever God allows in our lives is for a reason and a purpose under Heaven. When we become a Christian, God gives us His promises to always do what's best for our lives. When we place our trust in His promises, we have placed the control stick in His hand.

God never allows the circumstances in our lives to leave until we have learned the lessons we need to grow by. It seems that the longer we fight His will, the longer the trial remains.

There were many times I begged God to remove my knee problems, but it never happened. It wasn't because God didn't have the power to restore my knees. It was because God had a plan for me to grow through my weaknesses. He needed to refine me through the fire of His testing so I would come out of the fire and be renewed for His service.

A Loving Hand

"For I the Lord thy God will hold thy right hand, saying unto thee, Fear not; I will help thee." –Isaiah 41:13

We don't need to walk through the dark valleys of our lives alone. God is there and He will hold our hand until we are safely through.

There were times when I felt so alone because the dark moments of my circumstances became so difficult and overwhelming that I began to feel as though I was going through the roughest part of the storm.

The moments felt like I was trying to walk across a narrow log and below me was a deep, rushing river of circumstance, until I saw God's presence standing before me. As I saw myself looking into His face, the overwhelming feeling of fear began to leave and God began to softly speak and say, "Diane, if you will take my hand, I will lead you out of your circumstances to moments of peace and safety."

There were times when I felt as if the log I was crossing on became never-ending, but God did keep His word. Now

He has me on a different plateau so I can use what God has taught me to reach out and help others.

His Way of Escape

"There hath no temptation taken you but such as is common to man; but God is faithful, who will not suffer you to be tempted above that ye are able; but will with the temptation also make a way to escape, that ye may be able to bear it." –I Corinthians 10:13

God heals some people while He sustains others who are suffering to make His name known. Either way, God is in complete control as He brings His plan together for our lives so His master plan can be complete.

God knows how to make a way of escape for us through sustaining us or through a healing because He made an escape for us through His Son's death on the cross.

We can be going through extremely hard moments in our lives and feel as if we are the only one going through a difficult circumstance, but if we were to look at this world the way God sees this world, we would see a different picture.

God may not always be able to take us completely out of our circumstance, but He can take the edge off of your suffering by being there for you with encouraging words until He's ready to complete His way of escape for you.

Eagle's Wings

"But they that wait upon the Lord shall renew their strength; they shall mount up with wings as eagles; they shall run, and not be weary; and they shall walk, and not faint." – Isaiah 40: 31

Those who choose to follow God through hard times shall never lose strength for their journey. I faced many difficult circumstances and there were many times I wished that God would just take me home with Him, but His plans were not for me to come home.

There were many times that I found myself spiritually weaker because I was trying to make it through on my own instead of calling out to God for His strength.

God showed me that I couldn't just soak up what strength I had and expect to make it through my circumstance because when my small amount of strength is gone, I will have nothing to lean on and I'll begin to fall.

God taught me to seek Him deeper and find His perfect strength. He taught me that I could gain more strength from Him if I would look to Him instead of myself.

If we knew that there was a hidden treasure, we wouldn't look on the ground for the treasure; instead, we would dig deep below the surface to find the hidden treasure.

This story is very similar to how we find God's perfect strength. All we have to do is dig a little deeper with God. Once we find His strength, then we will be able to do anything.

Resting in God's Lap of Love

"Come unto me, all ye that labor and are heavy laden, and I will give you rest." –Matthew 12:28

When the road before you gets difficult and you've had enough, then give all your hurts and needs to God. He is already waiting for you with open arms.

When I am feeling overwhelmed, I sit down and close my eyes and meditate on God, and then I visualize an empty box before me. I take the empty box and I fill it with all my needs and, when I am finished, I place the lid on the box and lay the box in God's lap and then I turn around and walk away.

From there, God takes my needs and He nails them to His cross; He exchanges each need for a brand new strength and uses His perfect strength to sustain me until He can make a way for me to be free.

I've learned that if I give my needs to Him and then turn around and worry about them, then I have taken my needs away from God. God wants us to trust Him and have the faith to believe that all things are possible through Him.

Take your needs and lay them in the lap of His love, and He will exchange your needs for His perfect strength. In His time and way, He will free you from your needs.

Rooted in Jesus

"But the God of all grace, who hath called us unto his eternal glory by Christ Jesus, after that ye have suffered a while, make you perfect, stablish, strengthen, settle you." –I Peter 5:10

Our moments of suffering and pain can feel never ending at times. We begin to feel like the moments of pain have become our lot in life and we begin to feel like the light at the end of the tunnel is no longer there for us. God's purpose for suffering is not to walk away and leave us alone; His purpose is to make us more deeply rooted in Him.

If I wanted to go outside and plant tulips, I would have to plant the tulip bulbs at the right depth so they could grow strong. If I didn't plant the bulbs deep enough, then the stems wouldn't be strong enough to weather the storms.

This example is similar to what God wants for us. God has given us His word as a tool so we can dig deep and find His strength and truth to live by. If we are burrowed deep within His word and we are spending time with Him each day, we will be rooted deep enough in God and we will be able to make it through any storm we are facing.

Straight Ahead with God

"And thine ears shall hear a word behind thee, saying, This is the way, walk ye in it, when ye turn to the right hand, and when ye turn to the left." —Isaiah 30:21

When we are traveling with God, there may be times that we get off on the wrong pathway because Satan is deceiving us. Satan may try to detour us off God's pathway by tricking us so we will get caught up too much in ourselves, our circumstances, and our own way of thinking. From there, we find ourselves lost and away from God.

When we become lost and we can't find our way back to God, then God becomes our Shepherd. He knows when there is one missing from His flock. When He hears our cry, He seeks us out until He finds us. If we are too weak to follow Him back, He will carry us upon His shoulders.

Satan is always prowling around looking for some way to lead us away from God, like a lion that seeks to destroy a weak animal, so we shouldn't focus so deeply on our circumstances, because if we do, Satan can end up leading us down the wrong pathway. Instead, our focus should always remain on God. We need to have a clear view of God so He can lead us on that straight and narrow pathway which leads to Heaven.

The Fragrant Pathway

"All the paths of the Lord are mercy and truth unto such as keep his covenant and his testimonies." –Psalm 25:10

One of my favorite flowers are the lilies. They have such a beautiful fragrance and when I smell them, I think of Easter or springtime.

When we are on the right pathway with God, we will know it because everything that happens around us will tell us that God is near. His presence will pour out such a beautiful fragrance that will draw us to His pathway of truth and mercy.

When my husband took me to the Oregon coast I had never seen the Pacific Ocean before, but when we came closer to the ocean I knew that we were almost there because I could smell the salty water in the air. When we are experiencing God's presence, we begin to know that He is near, too, because we feel His peace surrounding us.

When we face feelings of frustration and confusion and there is no peace, these negative feelings should alert us to seek out God.

Seeking His Answers

"For I know the thoughts that I think toward you, saith the Lord, thoughts of peace, and not of evil, to give you an expected end." – Jeremiah 29:11

"And ye shall seek me, and find me, when ye shall search for me with all your heart." –Jeremiah 29:13

When we accept Jesus to come and live within us, we place Him in complete charge of our life. I believe that God has laid out the whole plan for our life, from birth to death. He already knew how He was going to use our life when we were born.

If God is holding the control stick for each of our lives, then why do we try to take control? How can we control our lives when we don't even know what the plan is for our lives?

God wants us to seek Him for the answers. If we only seek Him for a while and give up when the answers aren't there, we will never find what He desires to give us. If we continually pursue God, He will meet us there and crown each effort with His truth. Remember, God is the only one who holds the plans to your life.

Hope for the Weary

"I had fainted, unless I had believed to see the goodness of the Lord in the land of the living." –Psalm 27:13

Many times I've wondered, where would I be right now if I didn't have the hope of meeting Jesus one day in Heaven? There wouldn't be any hope or meaning in life without Him, and I wouldn't have any destination to aim for on this pathway I'm travelling.

When I'm going through a lot of pain, my home in Heaven becomes a reminder that there will come a day when this pain will cease, and I will meet my best friend (Jesus) for the first time. He will exchange this broken down body for a new one. What amazes me about Jesus is that He can care for me while He also cares for many others around the world at the same time.

When days of discouragement come, God seems to take me back to other moments of pain and heartache, reminding me how far I've come with His help and guidance. When I think of the moments I've been through, I seem to gain new strength so I can continue to move forward with God. His strength and the hope of Heaven cause me to rejoice within my heart.

Finding Real Love

"Confess your faults, one to another, and pray one for another, that ye may be healed. The effectual fervent prayer of a righteous man availeth much." –James 5:16

God can stop us from moving forward on His pathway if we have sin in our heart. It's so easy to get caught up in judging others. God showed me that if I'm judging others for their faults, I'm never going to be able to see their needs and pray for them.

One day, I was thinking about Hell and how final eternity in Hell will be. Here on earth, God gives us the opportunity to begin again when we make a mistake. Once a person enters Hell, there's no turning back. Can you imagine living for eternity in as horrible a place as Hell? Life in Hell will just keep going on and on, with no end in sight.

As I thought more on Hell, I began to wonder how many people will end up there because we were too busy judging them, instead of loving them and seeing their need to know Jesus.

Judging others is another way Satan deceives us. He knows that if we have our minds on other people's faults, then we will never be able to see the need of their heart. We need to stop Satan in his tracks so we will always be able to see the needs of others.

Peaceful Thoughts

"Finally, brethren, whatsoever things are true, whatsoever things are honest, whatsoever things are just, whatsoever things are pure, whatsoever things are lovely, whatsoever things are of good report; if there be any virtue, and if there be any praise, think on these things." —Philippians 3:8

We can either bring good or evil into our lives by the things we hear, say, and do. We may not always notice what we are bringing into our minds and hearts because we get so caught up in our everyday lives. We need to slow down and learn to identify the evil that lurks around us.

If I am always allowing my mind to take in the things that are of good report, I will always feel God's peace. If I am always allowing my ears to hear good things, I will be able to listen to God's voice. If I am always allowing my eyes to view good things, I will be able to see things in this world the way God sees them. Most of all, if I am always allowing myself to do what is right, God will always desire to help me, too.

When we make mistakes and we find ourselves in the clutches of Satan, I believe that God's desire for us is to rise above the moment of despair and begin to seek out the things that will bring God back into our lives.

He's My Rock

"The Lord liveth; and blessed be the rock; and let the God of my salvation be exalted." —Psalm 18:46

God has become a solid foundation when my foundation of circumstance gives way. At the moment I find myself falling in despair, God reaches down and He lifts me up to a higher plain.

The more I find myself praising Him during difficult times, the more He longs to help me. When I praise Him, then I am showing God that nothing is too hard for Him to do. I begin to see His power become greater than my circumstance and my faith causes me to soar above the evil that surrounds me.

Remember, Jesus is alive and He still reigns over all this earth. Turn to Him today and start singing praises to Him, especially during difficult times, and your praise will cause you to soar above your circumstance.

My Shepherd

"The Lord is my Shepherd; I shall not want." — Psalm 23:1

"Yea, though I walk through the valley of the shadow of death, I will fear no evil; for thou art with me; thy rod and thy staff they comfort me." — Psalm 23:4

"Surely goodness and mercy shall follow me all the days of my life and I will dwell in the house of the Lord forever." — Psalm 23:6

I have chosen a few verses from this famous chapter of the Bible. These are some of the verses that have helped me the most through trying times.

"The Lord is my shepherd; I shall not want," brings hope to my thoughts because Jesus is my shepherd and, as He watches over me and takes care of me, I have no need of anything because He will always provide for His very own.

"Yea, though I walk through the valley of the shadow of death, I will fear no evil; for thou art with me; thy rod and thy staff they comfort me." This verse has truly brought me a comforting spirit. Even though God took me through some painful valleys, He showed me that I had nothing to fear because He would always be there to comfort me as I walked through moments of heartache and pain.

"Surely goodness and mercy shall follow me all the days of my life; and I will dwell in the house of the Lord forever." As long as I choose to follow God, God's goodness will continually follow me the rest of my life. When my life comes to an end, I will dwell with Him forever in Heaven where there will never be any pain or suffering again.

Seasons to Live By

"To everything there is a season, and a time to every purpose under the heaven...a time to break down, and a time to build up." — Ecclesiastes 3:1, 3b

Just as God has given us seasons in a year, He also allows us to go through different seasons in our lives.

Springtime begins to bring new growth as buds begin to appear on the branches of trees and flowers. As summer takes over, the warmth of the sunshine allows the flowers and leaves on the trees to open up as beautiful colors display a fresh new appearance. After a long, hot summer, fall begins as the leaves die off in brilliant colors of reds, yellows, and oranges; then, as winter takes over, all of creation begins to sleep in preparation for spring again. The cycle continues as years continually pass by.

Just as God created these seasons to continually bring new growth upon the earth, God also allows different seasons to take place in our lives so He can bring forth new growth in us. The painful moments we go through may seem to make us feel dead inside, with no hope, but just as we wait for winter to end so spring can come, we, too, must wait on God until He is ready to bring us out of our winter of despair.

When God's time comes, He will bring us out of the season of despair and will allow the lessons we've learned to bring on new growth so He can be made beautiful through us.

Sorrow for Joy

"Therefore the redeemed of the Lord shall return, and come with singing unto Zion; and everlasting joy shall be upon their head; they shall obtain gladness and joy; and sorrow and mourning shall flee away." —
Isaiah 51:11

Some people are totally healed in this life so God's awesome power can be seen. Some, like me, still continue to go through pain, but I believe that God left me with a sample of pain so I will always be able to connect with others who go through pain and heartache.

Even though my left knee continues to worsen and my rod treats me like I'm a weathervane, I know that there will come a day when all who have chosen to follow God will be relieved of their suffering, for He will exchange our pain and heartache for His everlasting joy and gladness in Heaven.

When I see the trees blowing in the wind or when I feel a cool breeze upon my face, these moments continually remind me that God is alive and at work in all of us. These moments are just a sample of God's awesome power, but when the day comes that He returns for His own, we will begin to see the awesome presence of One so true.

Comforting Words

"I remember they judgments of old, O Lord; and have comforted my-self." —Psalm 119:52

God showed me that I could use His word as a tool to comfort and bring peace during the raging storms. The Bible isn't like a book that is read once and then placed upon a shelf. The Bible is full of words that can provide comfort, strength, peace, and hope.

The Bible contains stories of people who suffered hard and long for the cause of Christ and then, in the end, found freedom through God. When these stories are read, we don't feel so alone in our despair because we find a bond between the story and our circumstances.

When I was going through counseling for my sexual abuse, I would look up a verse that would relate to my moment of heartache and memorize the verse, burying the verse deep within my heart, so I could slowly draw on the words during moments of weakness.

When I read these stories, I began to realize that if the people from long ago could make it through hard moments of despair so could I. Our God is the same God that helped Job and others during those difficult moments so let God use His word to comfort and sustain you.

Rescued from Destruction

"Though I walk in the midst of trouble, thou wilt revive me; thou shalt stretch forth thine hand against the wrath of mine enemies, and thy right hand shall save me." —Psalm 138:7

When I read this verse, I saw a picture of myself while I walked through one of the darkest moments of my life. The moment began when my orthopedic doctor thought we were dealing with infection in my right knee.

There were times during the surgeries that I felt so overwhelmed. I felt like I was standing on the edge of a cliff and all there was before me was destruction. There were times that I couldn't even cry out to God because I felt such deep despair so I wrote in the steam on the shower curtain, "OH GOD, HELP!"

Within moments, I felt God reaching out to me. He was filling my thoughts with songs. As I sang the songs I began to listen to the words that were coming out of my mouth and I knew God's presence was there because the words seemed to be for me. As I continued to listen, the words began to flood my heart and mind with His beautiful peace.

Since that time, God has placed me on a firm foundation that's closer to Him, and whenever I feel pain, discouragement, or heartache, I know that He will be close by, and as He whispers His soft spoken words into my thoughts, I once more find comfort as He restores my broken heart and spirit.

A Settled Thought

"Let not your heart be troubled: ye believe in God, believe also in me." –John 14:1

One day, God spoke to my heart and said, "Diane, how is it that you believe in me, yet you do not believe in what I can do for you?" My thoughts began to race as His words began to overflow my mind. I felt as though I had just been hit by a lightning bolt.

As I continued to think more on His question, I felt as if I had just discovered something new for the first time and my eyes were now being opened to the truth. It's true; if we are Christians and we truly believe in God, why do we allow ourselves to get so caught up in our circumstances? When we are caught up in our circumstances, we have pushed God out and we have made our circumstances stronger than God. If we believe in God, we should also believe that He will walk with us and help us through our problems.

I began to learn that if I only believed in Him and didn't believe in what He can do, all He died for is in vain. God not only died for our sins, but He also died to free us from moments like these. When we only believe in His name and not what He can do, we have made Him powerless in our lives.

He Will Never Let Go

"Be strong and of good courage, fear not, nor be afraid of them; for the Lord thy God, he it is that doth go with thee; he will not fail thee, nor forsake thee." —Deuteronomy 31:6

God's love alone can cover any evil that tries to take control of our lives. I began to realize this one day as my husband and I were having devotions. That day, we learned that if fear and doubt become stronger than our love for God, we fall and drift away from Him; but when our love for God becomes greater, we are able to remain closer to Him.

When my love for God becomes strong, I feel as though I'm just outside of Heaven's gates. His love is a love that draws me so close to Him that nothing else matters. It's as though I'm gated in with His love and nothing, not even fear or doubt, can find its way through His perfect love.

Fear and doubt can place us into a deep pit of despair where Satan can use our feelings to take us out of the hands of God so he can take control.

When we have a close relationship with God and we truly love Him, we will automatically receive His perfect strength and courage, and we can use them as weapons to defend ourselves against Satan's attacks.

Better Days Ahead

"For I reckon that the sufferings of this present time are not worthy to be compared with the glory which shall be revealed in us." —Romans 8:18

God has had me on a pathway, and that pathway has been very difficult at times. Through each trying moment, God continually reminds me that I'm on the right pathway. He's shown me that each difficult moment I've faced had to be used so He could give me His strength to travel on.

Picture yourself traveling down a long road, and the destination God has for you is Heaven. When you first start out, the road looks clear with no problems ahead, and then you get a flat tire. After you make it through the trying moment, you start out again, and the road starts to get bumpy. When you think that you can't handle what has already happened, a tree falls across the road. As each trying moment continues to pile up, you become more tired and the hope you started out with begins to leave.

Then, out of desperation, you cry out to God. His still, small voice begins to whisper into your ear as He begins to say, "I will help you; please don't give up. You're almost there; once you have reached your destination, all of your journey will be behind you and then you can come and live with me forever in Heaven."

God wants us to know that we have come so far, and even though the journey has been difficult, He doesn't want us to give up. He wants us to know that if we truly believe in Him, there will come a day when we will be freed from all suffering. As we finish that last mile of the road, we will find our destination in Heaven.

Suffering So Jesus Can Be Seen

"And he said, Abba, Father, all things are possible unto thee; take away this cup from me; nevertheless not what I will, but what thou wilt."
—Mark 14:36

When Jesus was in the Garden of Gethsemane, He prayed and asked His Father if this cup or moment could be taken away from Him. Jesus knew that nothing was impossible for His Father in Heaven, but at the same time, Jesus wanted His Father's will to be done, not His. God is capable of doing anything in our lives, but at the same time, it has to be what He desires for us.

God has His own reasons why we suffer in our lives. Even though it's hard for Him to stand back and watch us suffer, sometimes the painful moments have to happen so that His great power can be seen through us.

As I look back, I praise God that He allowed all the painful moments to happen in my life because He has given me a greater wisdom that has become richer over the past years.

His will and His lessons have allowed God to become my dearest friend. I learned that either I was going to go through the fire and come out as gold, or I was going to sit in my "ashes of despair" and allow my life to be totally in vain.

Shackles for a Crown

"I have fought a good fight, I have finished my course, I have kept the faith; Henceforth there is laid up for me a crown of righteousness, which the Lord, the righteous judge, shall give me at that day; and not to me only, but unto all them also that love his appearing." –II Timothy 4:7-8

What beautiful words of hope God has given us! I have found in my own life that God never wastes what He does and He never leaves anything unfinished. As He becomes our closest friend by believing in Him, it's not His will to allow suffering to go on into eternity. There will come a day when God will take the shackles of pain or the shackles of heartache and exchange them for a crown of righteousness that we will receive in Heaven.

I have learned that being a Christian isn't always easy, but at the same time, it wasn't easy for Jesus to be beaten and have a crown of thorns thrust into His skull. It wasn't easy for Jesus to have His hands and feet nailed to a cross. It wasn't easy to take the whole weight of the world's sin upon His shoulders as He died for all of us.

If Jesus could go through such a horrible death just to say He loves us, then why can't we continue to fight the good fight so we can show Jesus that we love Him, too? Our suffering will never compare to the awful and painful moments He spent on the cross, but if we continue to press on, no matter what pathway is before us, one day we will be able to exchange the painful shackles for His crown.

No More Tears

"For the Lamb which is in the midst of the throne, shall feed them, and shall lead them unto living fountains of waters: and God shall wipe away all tears from their eyes." — Revelation

For so many years, God has caught every teardrop that has fallen from my eyes, but when I get to Heaven, God will wipe away every tear. There won't ever be any tears again.

Can you imagine a time and place when we will never shed a tear again? There will be no more suffering, so there won't be any more tears of pain and heartache. There will be no more death, so there won't be any moments of mourning. In Heaven, God will turn our tears of pain and mourning into eternal joy and gladness.

When I stop and think, it's hard to imagine a place with no tears because that's all we experience here on earth. When I think of a place where there will never be any tears of pain or heartache again, my mind begins to rejoice!

God has given us a glimpse of Heaven so we will always have hope. The moments we suffer through won't be forever.

When I think of eternity in Heaven, the moments we suffer here on earth have become only a few moments.

Dear Reader

Dear Reader,

God has a plan for each of our lives. No person is different or greater in the eyes of God. He has made each of us in a unique way so when He places us all together, His master plan becomes complete.

It's not always easy to understand why some people suffer more than others. Sometimes we find out the reason for our suffering in our lifetime through the different ways God uses our suffering for His plan. Sometimes we have to wait and God will sit down with us in Heaven and then He will give us the answers to our questions.

Until that day comes, when we are together with God in Heaven, He wants us to use our circumstances of suffering to become stronger so others will see Him more. God has given us two choices in life. We can either lean on God's powerful strength so we can rise above the circumstance, or we can sit in our "ashes of despair" and allow our weaknesses to take over until we lose complete control and lose God in the end.

One day while my husband and I were having devotions, God gave me something special to think on and I would like to share this thought with you. When we accept Jesus, He breathes His own life within ours. From there, it's our responsibility to allow His life to come out of us and touch others. If we don't, we suffocate His spirit within ours.

For such a long time, I felt that my life would become one long lifetime of suffering. I would die, having had no purpose in my life, but God began to show me something different.

As I began to come out of all the surgeries, counseling, drugs, and pain, God reminded me that when I accepted Him to come and live within my heart, then I was giving Him my permission to use my life in any way that would help others to see Him more clearly. I learned that if I walked away from God, then I was tying God's hands behind His back and allowing His spirit to suffocate within mine.

When God's spirit is seen in our lives, others we come in contact with will experience His presence, too. When we touch another person's life, they begin to feel something different that they've never experienced before and that's God!

As Christians, why can't we take the time to console a person who is hurting with a special Bible verse or go out of our way to stop in and visit with them? You never know; your visit may be the only visit they've had all week. God is seen when we share ourselves in an extraordinary way.

I don't believe that God will waste anything; I believe that He has planned for your life. God seems to place our lives in the right spot...at the right time. It's up to us to be alert enough so we can always hear His calling. If our minds are continually on ourselves or the world, there won't be any room for God to work His plan through us. Good and evil can't reside together. We will either live our life completely for God or this world. These are the only choices God gives us. Once we clean out the clutter in our hearts and minds, God will move in and use us according to His plan.

If you are a disabled reader, remember that God never allows your illness or handicap to become a waste either. It's amazing how God uses different disabilities to be of encouragement to others. You, of all people, can relate to others who have similar disabilities. Let God show you His plan for your life. "Disable" doesn't mean "not able" in God's vocabulary. You may never know when your life may change the life of another person. Let God use your weaknesses for Him so that His strength may be shown through you.

Just as God uses our lives so His beauty can shine forth, He will eventually finish what He's started in you. Sometimes we can feel that we will never be set free from our circumstances, but God promises us in Philippians 1:6 that, "Being confident of this very thing, that he which hath begun a good work in you will perform it until the day of Jesus Christ." You may feel that God has forgotten you, but He hasn't. He's just waiting for the right time…His time.

Most everyone has put a puzzle together in their lifetime. After dumping all the pieces of the puzzle onto the table, we start to look for all the flat pieces and corners. Once we've put the frame of the puzzle together, then we continually seek out the pieces that will bring the puzzle to completion. We can't take any piece we find and force the piece to fit where it doesn't belong because then the picture of the puzzle wouldn't be seen.

God works in a similar way with our lives. God sometimes has to stand back while our puzzle piece of life is being formed so we will fit into the right part of His master plan (puzzle).

If you don't know God or your pathway is crooked and you feel like you are always taking the wrong detour, it may be time to see where you are with God.

If you have never known where your pathway should start and you feel lost or the area around you seems unfamiliar, it may be time for you to look at the spiritual map (Bible) and ask God for directions so you can know where you are headed.

God brought a beautiful story to my thoughts one day and I would like to share this story with you. In the story, I began to see Jesus as He was walking down a long and lonely road to Calvary. He was carrying a very heavy cross and His body dripped with blood from the beatings that were placed upon Him. I began to follow right behind Him. I was weighed down with a heavy load of sins. As I approached Him, I began to tell Him about the load I was carrying. All He said was, "Follow Me," so I did.

As we approached a hill, there appeared to be two thieves, hanging on their crosses. As I drew closer, I saw the Roman soldiers throw Jesus onto His cross, which was lying on the ground. I could barely watch as the soldiers were hammering spikes into Jesus' hands and feet.

Once the soldiers had Jesus in place between the two thieves, I began to see the sky darken and lightning bolts shoot across the sky. I yelled up to Jesus and said, "What's happening?" He looked down at me and said, "I've become the complete sacrifice for the load of sins you've been carrying along with the sins of many." Then He said, "It is finished," and He hung His head and died. I began to feel different. I quickly looked behind me and the heavy load that I had carried for so long was no longer there.

As I walked away, I knew that I would never be the same again because Jesus had taken my heavy load of sin and nailed it next to Him on the cross. As He became the complete sacrifice, He took my load of sin upon His shoulders and exchanged my sins for a piece of Himself.

If you are lost and you are searching for the pathway that God has for you, then say this small prayer...

"Lord Jesus, I know that I am a sinner and until you save me, I'll be lost forever. I thank you for dying for my sins on the cross of Calvary. I forgive those who have sinned against me and, in return, I ask you to forgive my sins, too. Lord Jesus, I give you complete control of my life and I ask You to save me, love me, and use me for Your honor and glory. I now receive You as Lord and Savior of my life. In Jesus Christ's name...Amen!"

Now that God has placed you on the pathway He desires for you, let this small prayer become a tool that will bring guidance to you as you follow God. "Now that I am a child of God, teach me how to live for you so I can know how to have a close and personal relationship with You that I may lead others to you...Amen."

God doesn't want us to just know of Him; He wants us to really know Him. If you had a friend and your friend told you that they loved you, you wouldn't really know they loved you just by their words. You would want them to show you that they loved you by their actions, too. Words never come alive until action is shown.

God doesn't want us to just say we love Him. When we just speak the words and do not live the words, we are just wearing a sign above our forehead that says, "I'm a Christian." God wants to see our words come alive through a personal relationship with Him. God has a plan and purpose for each of our lives, but how are we going to know what He has for us if we don't seek Him in a deeper way. We either have all of Him or none of Him; there's no in between with God.

God has become my best friend and I know that He is always there for me. When I need Him, He has never walked away from me. Even though my pathway became difficult and painful at times, I can say that God's love never grew dim. He has become my sunshine by day and my moonlight by night. God remained close by even when the clouds in my sky became the darkest, and He did all of this to just say, "I love you, Diane."

Now I understand that God had to take me down a difficult and painful pathway before I could write this book or help others. I had to experience a taste of pain and heartache so I could find God and allow Him to work through me. As each tear fell throughout my life, I found my selfish desires begin to leave, and when God saw that I was to the level of faith He desired, He knew that He could use me as an instrument of love and bring others to Him.

While I've been working on this book, God showed me where I was at one time and where I am now, and I will never be able to send up enough praises to thank God for all He's done throughout my lifetime. God has truly opened up my eyes so I can understand and know why He allowed so much pain to enter into my life. He wasn't hurting me; He was just showing His love to me by helping me to become something better for Him.

Someday soon, I will finally walk the last mile on my pathway; I will reach my destination in Heaven. As I stand before Jesus, I will fall into the arms of One so true, the One who always stood beside me and never walked away, the One who became my best friend. I will recognize Him because He will be the One with the scars on His hands and feet.

As I begin to take in all the beauty that's surrounding me, I breathe a sigh of relief as tears begin to fall down my face. As I look up to Jesus He wipes my tears for the last time. He says, "Diane, I knew the pathway wasn't easy for I cried with you, too. It's all right now; it's all over my child. You will never suffer again."

He begins to loosen each shackle of pain and heartache and as He takes the shackles away, He exchanges them for a beautiful crown. As I walk into Heaven with Jesus, I suddenly begin to notice that I'm not limping anymore, and there is no more pain. The scars that marked my body for so many years are no longer there and the rod that stiffened up my leg is gone and now I'm able to run again. I fall to my knees for the first time as my eyes remain fixed on Jesus. As He gently lifts me up to my feet, He presents me with a beautiful, white robe.

As I begin to walk with Jesus, I turn around for the final time as Heaven's gates begin to close. I begin to realize that I have truly reached my destination in Heaven where I will never suffer with pain and heartache again. What about you? Where will your pathway end? The painful storms you're experiencing will never cease, and you will never find the rainbow of hope and all you've been so helplessly in need of until you find Jesus.

Notes

The Rainbow in the Storm

Notes

Notes

Notes

Testimonial

My name is Jennifer Caccavale. I am a thirty-seven-year-old single mother, a disabled one at that. I would like to sum myself up briefly for the readers. I was a drug addict on and off for over twenty-five years. I was in and out of extremely abusive relationships. I was verbally, emotionally, and sexually abused for the most part of my life.

I came to Jesus eleven years ago. Even though I was saved, and as white as snow in the Lord's eyes, I still battled many addictions on and off.

I had the pleasure of being one of the first to read this book. The stories may be different from yours or mine, but the emotions are all the same. Pain is pain and hurts are hurts. We all go through trials in life. Some of us handle them differently than others. I found Diane's stories to be so moving. I felt her pain page by page. Yet even through her pain she always managed to find a way to share hope with others. The strength that I felt reading every page just knowing that it was her faith that kept her strong. I know I have come a very long way with God. By reading Diane's book I can honestly say that I have so much more hope now. Just the way that she broke the verses down, and showed how she used them in her trials, made me look at those verses in a whole different light. I feel I have a new outlook of life just by reading how one very loving, caring, and spiritual woman handled all of hers!

Jennifer Caccavale

About the Author

Diane K. Chamberlain was raised in a small town in Michigan where she married a wonderful man, Keith. She was born with a congenital problem in both knees and went through many surgeries trying to correct the problem.

Little did she know that God had "branded" her at birth for such a moment as this. Many in this world grow up and go to school or college to get their education, but that's not what God had in store for her.

Diane's education for writing this book came from twenty-one painful knee surgeries, heartache from sexual abuse as a child, and the loss of many things in her life, including the loss of children. As each painful moment came and as each loving desire left, God was taking all that brokenness in her life, and He was piecing it all together like a beautiful puzzle to make this book what it is.

Visit Diane on her website www.diane-chamberlain.com